An Extraordinary
Charge Against a Clergyman

An Extraordinary Charge Against a Clergyman

The Biography of the
Reverend Edward Muckleston MA (1819–1913)

Janet Mackleston

The Book Guild Ltd

First published in Great Britain in 2020 by
The Book Guild Ltd
9 Priory Business Park
Wistow Road, Kibworth
Leicestershire, LE8 0RX
Freephone: 0800 999 2982
www.bookguild.co.uk
Email: info@bookguild.co.uk
Twitter: @bookguild

Typeset in 12pt Minion Pro

Printed and bound by CPI Group (UK) Ltd, Croydon, CR0 4YY

ISBN 978 1913551 070

British Library Cataloguing in Publication Data.
A catalogue record for this book is available from the British Library.

For my father
William (Bill) Mackleston (1925–2013)

Acknowledgements

I WOULD LIKE TO THANK MY SISTERS CAROL AND Judith, Colin Broughton and Dorothy Prior, whose proof reading and constructive feedback has been invaluable. Gill Blanchard for her excellent writing course, encouragement and feedback. The staff at the various county archives, especially those in Shrewsbury, Warwick and Worcester, for their invaluable support in helping me to locate the relevant documents and granting their permission to use selected images.

Dear Reader,

It was 1985, my father being about to retire, when we asked him if he had any outstanding ambitions. He told us he had two: one was to visit the pyramids and the other to trace his ancestry. The family story went that his grandfather had moved from Shrewsbury to Manchester, changed his name from Muckleston to Mackleston and that his family had once been wealthy. My sister had a lovely cruise down the Nile; I got something far better as I spent a lot of my free time with Dad, travelling around the country in the hunt for our elusive ancestors.

One of our earliest trips was to Shropshire Archives where we found the Muckleston Pedigree. This exquisite book contained hand-drawn and beautifully illustrated family trees and coats of arms going back to 1345. It had been created by Mary Louisa Muckleston in the latter half of the nineteenth century, making us wonder about the early family genealogist and the life she had lived. She had incorporated details of her own branch of the family, including her brother the Reverend Edward Muckleston. At this time, we had no reason to believe he was anything other than a respectable Victorian clergyman.

Although, over the years, we had found snippets of information which led us to believe there may have been more to his story; it was the advent of the internet and subsequent indexing of a wide range of newspapers which fully opened my eyes to his rather unbelievable behaviour and character. He was not beneath using his social position, wealth and even his vocation to gain advantages which led to scandals reported by the press of the day. Considering he was a man of the church, he appeared to care little about the impact his actions would have on others around him.

Newspaper reports led me to various archives to validate the information and even, on occasions, to add to the story. Although I have used a little poetic licence in the introduction to this biography, in imagining his thoughts on his situation, everything else is factual according to the newspapers and the archival material I have used, including the weather. I have written his story loosely in chronological order but on occasions have grouped similar incidents together to more clearly depict his character in different situations.

My father had passed away by the time I started fully researching and writing this story. Was it serendipity, divine intervention or my father continuing to contribute to the research from heaven, which caused me to stumble over an article reporting that an auction house had just sold a portrait of the Reverend Edward Muckleston? A little bit of detective work was carried out, the new owners located and, thanks to the purchase being made by my sister, this portrait now has pride of place over my fireplace. I often make a toast to his portrait, saying who would ever had thought you were such a rogue?

There are other equally interesting characters in the Muckleston family whose stories I may one day also share, but for now I do hope you get as much enjoyment and surprise from reading his life story, as I did in researching and writing.

Janet Mackleston

Contents

Glossary of Terms

Advowson	The right to present to the bishop a fit person to fulfil a vacancy in the church. The bishop has the right to decline. A form of property which can be bought or sold.
Bailiff	The farm bailiff is employed by the owner and carries out the management of the farms, including collecting rents and supervising farm operations and labourers.
Benefice	A permanent appointment, typically of a vicar or rector, for which property and income are provided in exchange for carrying out parish duties.
Billhook	A traditional cutting tool used widely in agriculture.
Burgess	A freeman of a borough.
Chancel	The part of the church near the altar reserved for the clergy and the choir.
Churchwarden	Either of the two elected lay representatives in an Anglican parish, formally responsible for movable church property and for keeping order in church.
Cinque Cento style	A style of architecture, painting and design popularised by the High Italian Renaissance in the sixteenth century.
Convocation	A group of people formally assembled for a special purpose.

Copyhold	Land held according to the custom of the manor, taking its name from the fact that the title deed received by the tenant was a copy of the relevant entry in the manorial court roll.
Court of Chancery	Presided over by the Lord Chancellor and his deputies. People turned to this court as it was seen to be more merciful, not bound by the strict rules of other courts, and was therefore able to deal with more complicated cases.
Curate	An assistant to the vicar, rector or parish priest.
Equity of redemption	The right to redeem the property on payment of the principal, interest and costs.
Glebe	An area of land within the parish used to support the parish priest.
Incumbent	The holder of an office or post.
Indenture	A legal agreement, contract or document.
Jointure	An estate settled on a wife for the period during which she survives her husband.
Litigious	Tending or too ready to take legal action to settle disputes.
Liturgy	A set form in which Christian public worship is conducted.
Living	An income sufficient to live on or the means of earning it.
Matriculating	The process of formally becoming a student.
Messuage	A dwelling house with outbuildings and land.
Nave	The central aisle of a church.
Offertory	A collection of money made at a religious service.
Ordination	A ceremony bestowing a person with a position of religious authority.
Paten	A plate, typically made of gold or silver, used for holding the bread during the Eucharist.
Perpetual curate	A clergyman who officiated in a parish, but unlike vicars and rectors, their income did not derive from the possession of tithes.
Plaintiff	A person who brings a case against another in a court of law.

Promissory note	A signed document promising to pay a stated sum by a stated date or on demand.
Reredos	An ornamental screen covering the wall at the back of an altar.
Sequestrator	Someone who takes possession of a property for a time to satisfy a demand out of its rents or profits.
Surrogate	A substitute.
Threepenny bit	A coin which equalled three old pence.
Tithes	One tenth of annual produce or earnings, formerly taken as a tax to support the church and clergy.

MONETARY COMPARISONS

Figures given in square brackets [ ] are supplied for comparison purposes. The National Archives currency converter has been used to compare the monetary amounts of yesteryear with those of 2017. It must, however, be remembered that this comparison is an estimate for general inflation, and house price and wage inflation figures would be different.

Family Tree of Edward Muckleston

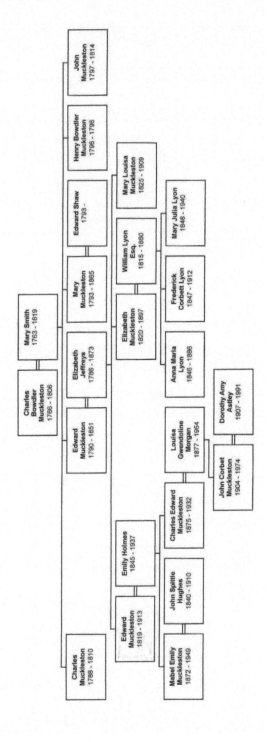

Introduction

5 June 1875
Solihull Police Court

EDWARD SAT WITH HIS HEAD IN HIS HANDS; ALL HE could do now was wait. Wait for those two magistrates to decide his fate. He had prayed that they would understand that he had simply made a mistake and dismiss the case, but he had seen the look on their faces when they had heard that he had been convicted of the same offence before. The best he could now hope for was that they would decide his punishment did not warrant a prison sentence. Yes, he had faced the possibility of time in prison before, most notably over the incident with the trees fifteen years ago, but then he had money and there was the alternative of a fine which he had been able to pay. Prison would not only mean the loss of his freedom and incarceration in a place he could hardly bring himself to think about but also the loss of his job and his home, and what would happen to Emily and the unborn baby.

At least his father was not around to see his beloved only son, of whom he had been so proud, brought so low in life. Edward had been blessed with so much and was now on the verge of losing everything. His fate was in the hands of those two magistrates.

He sat up straight; now was not the time to be seen showing weakness. He glanced at the empty chair next to him, one in which his solicitor should have sat, but he had been unable to find anyone willing to represent him and he had conducted his own defence. Familiar as he was of court procedure, experience gained over many years, he had been comfortable conducting the cross-examination. Glancing around the packed courtroom, his eyes settled on his accusers, the railway employees and their solicitor. In the centre of the group stood Inspector Ledbrooke, the man who had ruined him once before and who was trying to do so again, all to enhance his own reputation.

His eyes moving amongst the crowd, not surprisingly, he saw the reporter from the *Leamington Spa Courier* who had travelled the fifteen miles to observe this case being heard in Solihull and who had obtained a front-row seat. The newspaper had frequently reported on the challenges that Edward had faced ever since settling in Haseley ten years earlier; sensational headlines ensuring that all his friends, neighbours and acquaintances knew all about the difficulties he faced, their reporting often being picked up by other newspapers, spreading the news far and wide. He could see the headlines now: 'An Extraordinary Charge Against a Clergyman'.

Chapter One

A Privileged Upbringing

THE CRIES OF A NEWLY BORN BABY GIRL RANG OUT along the corridors of Kensington Palace in London. It was Monday 24 May 1819 and Alexandrina Victoria, the daughter of Prince Edward, the Duke of Kent, and his wife, Princess Victoria of Saxe-Coburg-Saalfeld, had made her entrance into the world.[1] Less than a week later, on Sunday 6 June, over 150 miles away in an imposing street in the centre of Shrewsbury, similar cries were heard at the birth of a boy who was to be named Edward. He was the son of 'Captain' Edward Muckleston, an army officer who had retired on half pay, and his wife, Elizabeth née Jeffreys. This boy's father was a member of an ancient, wealthy, landowning Shropshire family who could trace their ancestry in the county back to the fourteenth century; his mother was an heiress in her own right. Although his father had only ever reached the rank of lieutenant, he styled himself as a captain, fabrication being a personality trait which he would pass on to his son. The lives of neither of these babies would turn out as their parents could have anticipated at the time of their births. Alexandrina Victoria would become the great Queen Victoria and Edward would become a clergyman, a great admirer of the Queen and one who would one day commission a memorial to her.

Dogpole, the street in which the family lived, was situated in the parish of St Mary's and it was at this church that Edward was baptised a month after his birth.[2] He was to have two siblings: Elizabeth, born the following year,[3] and Mary Louisa, who arrived when Edward was almost six years old.[4]

Like all towns in the early and mid-nineteenth century, Shrewsbury was dirty and overcrowded, and in 1821, an Act of Parliament created a body of men called Improvement Commissioners with powers to pave, clean and light the streets of the town. Despite the developments, around the time of the birth of Mary Louisa, the family decided to move to Bicton House, a country estate which included a large, square, red-brick house of three storeys. It had been built twenty-five years earlier and was surrounded by acres of land. The move provided a healthier environment for the children and allowed Edward senior to lead the life of a country squire. Situated three miles north-west of Shrewsbury, the estate was rented from Henry Benyon[5] at a cost of £100 per year [equivalent to approximately £6,000 today].[6]

Edward junior was a much-loved son, evidenced by the entries in his father's household account books which recorded him as 'dear Edward'; the daughters did not warrant a mention. The family lived well at Bicton; there was regular expenditure on delicacies such as oysters, oranges and figs, and the wine supplier and butcher's bills were significant. Edward senior regularly purchased livestock, including lambs, cows and bullocks – most likely for the home farm – and there was also a pony for the children in 1827. No expense was spared on material for dresses for their mother; as members of the gentry, they had a busy social life. The family also employed several servants, who occupied the servant's quarters.[7]

Edward senior believed that education was very important and he engaged a private tutor named Mr Case to teach his son between the ages of nine and twelve, thereby providing Edward junior's early schooling.[8] He then entered Shrewsbury School in 1832 at age thirteen, the minimum age to join the school, and is recorded as leaving just before his nineteenth birthday.[9] Edward junior was educated under the famous headmasters, Dr Samuel Butler and Dr Benjamin Hall Kennedy. During the headmastership of Dr Butler, the school's reputation rose dramatically, and the standard of its scholarship was the equal of any other public school in England. He set older boys in authority over the younger ones but turned a blind eye to the bullying and, on average, seventy fights that occurred each week which were considered character-building. It is said that Dr Butler was disliked by one of the school's most famous pupils, Charles Darwin, who attended the school ten years prior to Edward. Darwin felt that the range of subjects taught at the school was too narrow. Dr Kennedy, who succeeded Dr Butler in 1836, maintained the high standard of education but also broadened the academic syllabus.[10] Meanwhile Edward's father continued to engage tutors to supplement the education that he was receiving at the school.

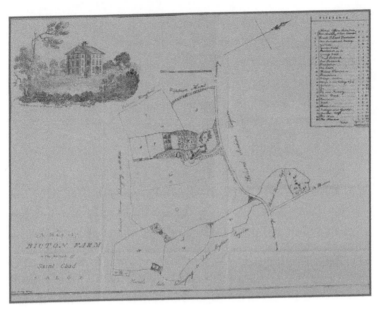

Sales particulars for Bicton House and farm.

Edward was in his final year at Shrewsbury School when, on the death of her uncle, King William IV, Victoria became Queen of Great Britain and Ireland.

In 1835, the family were given notice to quit Bicton House, as Henry Benyon wished to sell it. Afterwards the family rented another property owned by the Benyon family in Shrewsbury at number 2 Quarry Place. Their new home was situated in the fashionable south-western part of the town and overlooked the old quarry next to the River Severn. The site had been converted into a twenty-nine-acre park which had been landscaped with walks where the genteel folks of Shrewsbury would promenade. This conflicted with those who used the river for its traditional purpose, such as bathing and washing clothes. Many men would bathe and swim naked, and this was not a sight that the gentry of Shrewsbury wished to see on their daily walks.[11] Edward's boarding school was in Castle Gates, near the castle, also in the town centre, and at least now his family were only a short walk away.

As a young man, Edward junior tended to be lazy, as a letter written by his father to Mary Louisa on 18 November 1836, when Edward senior was away from home on army business, reveals: 'I received your letter yesterday, I was extremely happy to receive so favourable account of your dear brother, which will enable him to pursue his studies and as his time is of the greatest consequence it will be of the utmost importance for him not to lose a moment and I feel confident now he is to come to a desirable age, he sees the value of time in the same light that I do and will employ it to his future advantage in this life.' His first thoughts were clearly for his seventeen-year-old son and heir as, after exhorting his daughter to bathe more frequently as her body odour displeased him, he went on to say, 'you must also impress it on your brother to be very careful not to take cold, as it may make him very wretched and uncomfortable all winter'.[12] It would normally be down to the mother to deal with the children's cleanliness and it seems a bit unfeeling to put such a comment in a letter.

A recent photograph of 1 and 2 Quarry Place with the three-storey red-bricked home of the Muckleston family on the right, built c1791–1793 for the Benyon family.

Edward's early education stood him in good stead, as he went on to attend Worcester College at Oxford University, matriculating on Thursday 28 February 1839 aged nineteen.[13] In the early nineteenth century the predominate studies at Oxford were Theology and Classics, and Edward had a cousin, once removed, called Rowland Muckleston, eight years his senior who had also attended Worcester College. Rowland had entered the college in 1830 and three years later gained a first-class honours degree in Classics followed in 1836 by a master's degree. He had been ordained in 1837 but chose to remain at Oxford as an academic and went on to become a Doctor of Divinity. A year after his ordination, Rowland had been made Master of the School and in the following year, when Edward joined the college, was appointed Dean and Vice Provost, a position he held until 1856.[14] This family connection may have helped Edward's application, their common ancestor being John Muckleston (1731–1782), a gentleman of Merrington near Shrewsbury, an estate the family had held since 1615. John was Rowland's grandfather and Edward's great-grandfather. Rowland's father was also a clergyman and, as this was Edward's career choice, he may have hoped to use the family relationships to obtain a position in his chosen vocation.

If family connections had indeed helped Edward to gain entry to the college, it does not appear to have helped him to gain his qualification. It took him six years, twice as long as normal, to achieve his first degree, which was conferred on him on Friday 25 April 1845.[15] The reason for this is unclear but it is possible that he had an illness, there may have been family issues, although I am unaware of any; or was it the case that he simply struggled with the required studies? Family or not, Rowland was clearly not going to grant a degree until his cousin had met the academic requirements. Things were to improve as, after further study, it only took Edward the standard two years to achieve a master's degree, which he finally received four days after his twenty-eighth birthday, thus completing his university education.[16] Proud of his achievement, he would always refer to himself as Edward Muckleston MA, possibly feeling superior to those without such a high level of academic gain.

During the years Edward had been completing his university education, Victoria had married her cousin Albert and now had five children.

Whilst his son was away at university, Edward's father purchased the house in Quarry Place from its owner, Samuel Yate Benyon, for £1,200 [around £85,000 today]; he did not immediately have this sum of money and also needed £100 [about £7,000 today] for other purposes, and so on the same day mortgaged the property to Dr Robert Darwin (Charles Darwin's father) for £1,300 at four per cent interest.[17] Such personal loans and mortgages were very common, and a means of investment for the lenders. The Darwin's solicitor and financial adviser, Thomas Salt, lived across the road at 6 Quarry Place and it could be assumed that he recommended the transaction. Eighteen months later,[18] Edward's father had repaid the debt, plus the interest, and the mortgage was cleared.[19]

Edward was still at Oxford when he reached the age of twenty-one. This meant he had full rights of citizenship and he took the opportunity to be admitted as a burgess, or freeman, of Shrewsbury.[20] Many of his ancestors had been burgesses; usually from the upper echelons of local society, they were property owners or traders who, as well as being granted voting rights, were given a share in the corporate property of the town. In exchange for these rights, burgesses were expected to pay rates for the upkeep of Shrewsbury. Involvement in town affairs was not a priority for Edward; after spending all those years on education it was now time for him to make his own mark on the world.

Chapter Two

Ordination

O N   A   C O L D   A N D   F R O S T Y   M O R N I N G ,   F I V E   D A Y S
before Christmas Day 1846, Edward was ordained
a priest by John Lonsdale, the Bishop of Lichfield. The
ceremony took place in the Bishop's Chapel at Holy Trinity
Church in the small agricultural market town of Eccleshall
in Staffordshire.[21] The same bishop had ordained Edward
as a deacon earlier that same year. This ceremony saw
many other fellow clergymen appointed to the diocese; in
total thirteen deacons and eighteen priests were ordained
on this day.[22] It would be nice to imagine that his proud
parents and sister Mary Louisa would have made the
thirty-mile carriage ride to watch the ceremony, but it is
more likely that it was a private event. His sister Elizabeth
had married some eighteen months earlier and had a three-
month-old daughter to care for. Since his ordination as a
deacon, Edward had been working as a curate to the parish
of Welsh Hampton in Shropshire, also part of the diocese
of Lichfield, a position he was to hold between 1846 and
1848.[23] The vicar of this parish was the Reverend Henry
Cornwall Legh, who would have been responsible for

Edward's initial training as a clergyman, a process which normally took about a year, and once Reverend Legh was confident that Edward was ready he would recommend him to the bishop for ordination as a priest. While he was undergoing this training, Edward was also completing his second degree at Oxford.

The first step to becoming ordained was to obtain an honours degree from Oxford or Cambridge universities and Edward would also have required a testimonial from his college saying that he was a suitable candidate for the clergy. He would then present this to a bishop who would carry out an examination to confirm he was competent in Latin, knew the scripture, and was familiar with the liturgy and church doctrine. At this time Edward's father was a Justice of the Peace for Shropshire and his high profile within the county may have helped Edward to gain the position at Welsh Hampton, or the bishop himself may well have felt that he would be a suitable assistant to Reverend Legh. Edward had been working as curate to this parish for a least nine months prior to his ordination as a priest. In March 1846 he conducted his first baptism; continuing to learn his craft from Reverend Legh, he conducted his first burial on 2 June and was reading banns and entering them into the register from August. During the following year he appears more frequently in the registers and had clearly taken on a greater role within the parish.[24]

Edward's life as a curate would not have been easy. During the Victorian era, as many as half the ordained priests did not have a living and became curates who basically deputised for, and were paid by, the vicar. Some incumbents employed curates immediately and others only when they felt the need to retire. The pay was poor, typically

£50 per year [equivalent to our modern minimum wage] and, as the vicar often retained the vicarage as a home, the curate also had to find his own accommodation close to the church. He could lose his position at any time and there was plenty of competition for these appointments. Although, as members of the Church, they were classed as gentlemen, their role was subservient and poorly paid, and curates were often held in low regard. This was Edward's situation in 1846, but he would have had high hopes of a parish of his own eventually.

Traditionally within the Muckleston family, the eldest son had normally inherited the bulk of the family fortune. Second sons may have inherited some dower lands from their mothers, but for younger sons there was often little wealth to pass on. Becoming a clergyman, a doctor, a lawyer or joining the army as an officer, were professions befitting a gentleman and were viable options to inheriting wealth. Why Edward chose to enter the Church is not known, as he was an only son and would expect to inherit from his father. He may have had a calling, but the family fortunes in this branch of the family, although still substantial, were dwindling and it may have been prudent to have a career as a way of earning an additional income. In Edward's case, joining the clergy would prove to be a shrewd decision.

There was also a greater demand for clergymen, as in 1818 the government had voted to allocate one million pounds for new churches to be built, followed in 1824 by a further half a million pounds. Between 1851 and 1875, this money was used to build 2,348 new churches, and this meant there were opportunities for those wishing to earn their living in this manner.[25] The number of clergymen rose from 14,500 in 1841 to 24,000 in 1875. Things were also changing within the Church, as during this period there was a rise in new Protestant denominations such as Methodists, Baptists and Quakers, with almost half of the church-going population visiting non-Church of England places of worship.

Whether a curate or a vicar, the clergy were heavily involved in parish life. As well as holding the Sunday services and Holy Communion, a clergyman would carry out baptisms, marriages and funerals. Duties would also include the day-to-day running of the parish, which included visiting the sick and officiating at parish meetings. These meetings would cover local issues, including the administration of the Poor Laws, collection of the poor rates, care of the poor, maintenance of the church, appointment of churchwardens and Surveyors of the Highways, who supervised the maintenance and repair of the roads.

Welsh Hampton was a beautiful village in the northern part of Shropshire, close to the Welsh border, three miles east of Ellesmere and eighteen miles from the family home in Shrewsbury. In 1841 there were 118 inhabited houses and 560 inhabitants and covered an area of just under 3,000 acres. One of the main landowners within the parish were the executors of the Earl of Bridgewater, an unmarried eccentric member of the Egerton family who had died in 1826 and whose lands were held in trust.[26] Edward would later claim that he had been chaplain to Lady Ellesmere, wife of the Earl of Ellesmere, another member of the Egerton family. If this was indeed true, it is likely that he undertook this appointment whilst working in this parish.

During November 1847, Reverend Legh was to pass away at his parsonage in Welsh Hampton, he was just thirty-six years old.[27] Edward continued to carry out parish duties after his former employer's death, his last entry in the registers being a baptism which he conducted on 30 January 1848. By 6 February the new vicar, the Reverend George S. Masters, had taken up parish duties and, as he did not require a curate, Edward, at twenty-eight years old, was unemployed.[28]

Probably to give Edward a level of financial independence and knowing how difficult it was at that time to obtain positions within the Church, Edward's father arranged for him to receive the rents from some properties he owned.[29] These properties were situated in Coton Hill in Shrewsbury, where there were fifteen rent-paying tenants, plus a farm in Llanfihangel in Cardiganshire known as Perry Bank. These premises had formed part of his mother's marriage settlement and, as a condition of this transfer of lands, Edward agreed to a jointure which stated that, should his mother survive her husband, he would pay her £160 a year [around £13,000 today] arising from these properties.[30]

More than eighteen months after leaving Welsh Hampton, on 24 November 1849 Edward's appointment to the rural parish of Mackworth in Derbyshire was announced in the *Oxford University and City Herald* newspaper. Lying on the banks of the river Derwent with a population of just 561,[31] as with Welsh Hampton this parish came under the diocese of Lichfield.[32] Often clergymen were licensed by the bishop to work anywhere within the diocese and this was probably the case with Edward. Although he may have carried out other duties on behalf of the vicar, Reverend George Pickering, such as the Sunday sermons and visiting the sick, the registers indicate that the only services he undertook were a couple of burials in the last two months of 1849. Whether it was planned to be a temporary appointment or if there was some other reason is not known, but in January 1850 Edward was succeeded as curate by Reverend Gilder. The information Edward would subsequently give to those compiling the clergy lists indicates that he was in Mackworth from 1848 to 1850 where, in truth, records show his time here was little more than three months.

A month prior to taking up his post at Mackworth, Edward had travelled north up the British Isles, past Inverness to Cromarty, a coastal town, in the Scottish Highlands. A long and tiring journey, he probably used the newly emerging railways and mail coaches. The reason for his visit was to conduct the wedding of Major Angus McKay of the 21st Royal Fusiliers to Mary Magdalene Poyntz. Mary was the daughter of Major Sir George Gun Munro fourth Laird of Poyntzfield House in Cromarty, which is where the wedding took place on the 25 October.[33] It is unclear as to why an English priest was chosen to conduct the service; Edward could have been a friend of the groom or the connection could have been through his father, who may have known Major Munro from his army days. Edward was to make many visits to Scotland during his lifetime and in his later years he would also become a director of a business owned by the Munro family. It therefore seems likely that there was a close friendship.

Following his few months at Mackworth, Edward travelled four miles further east into Derbyshire and

took on the curacies of
Chaddesden and, a few
miles further north, the
parish of Stanley.[34] The
combined population
of the two parishes was
just under 800 souls.
While working as
curate in Chaddesden,
shortly after the start of

*Poyntzfield House – from a
postcard dated 1906.*

the new year in 1851, Edward was the victim of a fraud
carried out by what the newspapers called, 'an artful
scamp'. A man had called at Edward's home and told a
clever tale about how he had been out of work but had
been offered a job by a tradesman in Belper as a tailor. He
claimed to have walked a great distance in the search for
work, but his wife was no longer able to continue, and he
wanted to borrow a few shillings to hire a cart to convey his
wife and family. Edward gave him the required sum but on
calling on Reverend Gilder at Markeaton, found that the
same person had visited him only a couple of hours before
with 'the same sorry tale'.[35]

At the beginning of 1851, the perpetual curacy of
the small parish of Acton Round in Shropshire, became
vacant. Oxford University was responsible for filling this
permanent post, and a position back in his home county,
with a regular income, may have been ideal for Edward.
Confusion then ensued, with some newspapers reporting
that Edward had been appointed to this parish.[36] However,
the *London Evening Standard* went on to report that
a convocation had been held on 14 February so that an
election could be held to decide who would be appointed

to Acton Round, saying, 'There being only one candidate, namely the Reverend Dr Day, a graduate of Trinity College, Dublin, that gentleman was declared by the Senior Proctor to have been duly elected.' A fortnight later the same newspaper reported that, 'The university seal was affixed to the presentation of the perpetual curacy of Acton Round, in favour of the Reverend William Godfrey Day.'[37] Reverend Day was indeed appointed and was at Acton Round until his death a couple of years later.[38] As late as 1 March it was still being reported in some newspapers that Edward had been elected to the perpetual curacy, and whether he wanted the position or not, it may have been a confusing time for him.

Edward was working in Chaddesden and Stanley for just over a year,[39] but by May 1851 he had made the decision to retire from his curacies and the local newspaper reported on his retirement, saying, 'On Sunday last after the congregation having participated in the high and holy duties of prayer and praise, he delivered his valedictory address, selecting for his text the 9th verse of the 3rd chapter of Ezekiel. The reverend gentleman in the course of an orthodox and impressive sermon, gave a summary of the duties and privileges of the clergy and laity, and earnestly exhorted his hearers to continue in communion with Christ's Holy Church in these days of trial.'[40] It is unclear what Edward meant by 'days of trial', but he was clearly 'high church'. Clergymen who were 'high church' were more ritualistic when conducting their services; those who were 'low church' tended to be more evangelistic in their approach.

His departure from Derbyshire coincided with the opening of the Great Exhibition, which took place in the purpose-built Crystal Palace; devised by Prince Albert, it was opened by his wife Queen Victoria. Lasting over five months, the exhibition was designed to allow countries from all over the world to showcase their achievements. It became the first of a series of world fairs which attracted many famous faces, including Darwin and renowned writers of the time, such as Charles Dickens and Lewis Carrol. Six million people, a third of the population of Great Britain at that time, were said to have attended.

Although Edward could well have been looking for another position at this time, little did he know that his family was about to need his support.

Chapter Three

Inheritance

O N SATURDAY 21 JUNE 1851, EDWARD'S FATHER suddenly passed away at his home at Quarry Place; he was sixty-one years of age.[41] The reason for his death, given by the surgeon Edwin Foulkes, was apoplexy a term at the time used to denote a sudden death. Three days after this sad event, George Newnes, Edward senior's twenty-two-year-old valet, registered the death, stating that he was present at the time.[42] Only a week before, Edward senior had been carrying out his duties as a magistrate and had committed James Jones, a labourer of Little Ness, to six weeks' hard labour for poaching at Great Ness.[43] He left no will, which was surprising as he was an organised person who kept detailed household accounts and was paymaster for the army regiment he had belonged to. His widow Elizabeth applied to administer his estate and his personal property was recorded as being valued at under £3,000 [which is about the equivalent of a quarter of a million pounds today].[44] There were houses, cottages and land in the townships of Bromlow and Worthen, and rights belonging to the manor of Aston Rogers, as well as properties in Shrewsbury, all of which now fell to his son, Edward, as the only male heir. Being free from parish duties, Edward was able to support his mother in the administration of the estate.

Edward Muckleston senior was buried in the family crypt at St Chad's Church in Shrewsbury.[45] St Chad's had been built in 1792 to replace another church of that name on a different site and Edward's father had been a senior churchwarden in the new church which was only a short distance from his home at Quarry Place. This building had a distinctive round shape and high tower.

As Edward senior was still on half pay from the army at the time of his death, his widow Elizabeth was able to apply for a widow's pension,[46] she also had the income of £160 per year from the lands she brought to the marriage as had previously been agreed with her son. Being single, Edward would require a hostess and his mother was well placed to carry out this duty for him. Edward's sister Mary Louisa, now twenty-six years old, would remain unmarried and dependant on her mother's and brother's goodwill.

On 14 June 1845, one day before drawing up a marriage settlement for his eldest daughter Elizabeth, Edward's father had borrowed £1,000 [approximately £70,000 today] from Charles Darwin, the naturalist and author of *On the Origin of Species* and *Descent of Man*, at an interest rate of three and a half per cent, the lower

St Chad's Church, Shrewsbury.

rate often given to those he particularly trusted.[47] This loan had been arranged, once again, through his neighbour Thomas Salt and it was secured on a commercial property at 82 Wyle Cop, Shrewsbury, the house at Quarry Place still having a mortgage on it at the time.[48] The money had been taken from Emma Darwin's trust fund and the loan, which was for five years, was already overdue and they now wished to foreclose. Emma was Darwin's wife and the youngest of the seven children of Josiah Wedgwood.

Six months after Edward senior's death, Darwin had written to Thomas Salt, saying:

'I yesterday sent a note to M^r. Jos. Wedgwood to be forwarded to you (if he consented), asking you to give notice to the Ex^s: of the late Capt. Muckleston to pay the 1000£: but now this large sum of 10,000£ is to be paid up, I do not wish for Capt. Muckleston's thousand, without you think it likely that it will in any case be soon paid up, for in that case, I should like it soon. If, however, you suppose that this 1000£ will be kept for some years, please burn my note, & let the affair rest as it is. P.S. I have opened my letter to say, that upon further reflexion, I will request you to be so good as to give notice to Executor of Capt. Muckleston, if you receive (as I anticipate) M^r. Jos. Wedgwood's consent.'[49]

A very indecisive Darwin; having received the payment of another loan, he had changed his mind about asking for the money from Edward and then, even before he sent the letter, had changed his mind once again and decided he did want it after all.

It is unlikely that Edward knew that Darwin was close to allowing him more time to pay off the debt, but he was certainly in no hurry to make the repayment. Two years after asking him to settle his father's debt, the lenders decided to put Edward under pressure, and he was given six months to pay back the money plus interest or he was told they would take the property.[50] The Wyle Cop property was at that time occupied by William Price, a wine merchant, and his undertenants William and Charles Hewlett, cabinet makers and upholsterers. A further letter sent to Edward, dated 1 May 1854, indicates that the money owed was to be paid before the end of the month; however, letters in the Darwin archives show that it wasn't until 11 July 1854 that the loan was settled.[51]

Edward had been challenging to deal with and Darwin wrote to Thomas Salt, saying, 'I am much obliged to you for your note received this morning, informing me that 1018£ will be paid to my account this day in London.— I am very sorry that you sh[d]. have been inconvenienced by Mr. Muckleston paying the whole in Gold.— I am thankful to have done with the gentleman.' Edward's mother had made the payment in gold coins, a hurried method of payment when the prospect of foreclosure is at last taken seriously, but knowing his personality, in this instance, it looks as if Edward was being deliberately uncooperative.

Edward was not short of money, as he had commissioned a window to honour his father. This was placed in St Chad's where his father was buried and is the only non-religious window in the church. The handsome window had been created by Shrewsbury craftsman Mr David Evans. It was placed in the eastern side of the church and was described in local newspapers: 'The glass is in the Cinque Cento style and contains in the centre the armorial bearings of the deceased gentleman (who was an old and highly respected inhabitant of the parish), surrounded by rich ornamental glass of the most harmonious colouring.' His father's date of birth and death are included in the window.[52] The left-hand

The Muckleston Window in St Chad's Church, Shrewsbury.

side of the armorial bearings show the Muckleston family crest of greyhound heads and crosses and on the right-hand side that of his heiress wife, the Jeffreys family. The family motto of *fideliter*, meaning faithfully, also forms part of the window.

Edward, now thirty-two years old, was head of the family and a landed proprietor with a desirable house in Shrewsbury, although he also had a widowed mother and unmarried sister to support. All Edward needed now was a good position within the Church.

Chapter Four

Appointed to Ford

THE DEATH OF HIS FATHER HAD CATAPULTED Edward from lowly curate, constantly seeking a position, to the echelons of the landed gentry. As well as owning land and property throughout Shropshire, he was now also Lord of the Manor of Aston Rogers, a hamlet south-west of Shrewsbury.

Less than six months after his father's death, he was appointed Vicar of St Michael's, the parish church in the small village of Ford, giving him the secure position within the church which he had been looking for. The living was in the gift of George Tomline Esq, a former MP of Shrewsbury[53] and was a permanent post with a small but regular salary in excess of £100 per annum [about £8,000 today] and just five miles from his home in Quarry Place. This position was more secure than his previous curacies as only a bishop could remove a vicar from his living and then only with good reason.

Ford was a small but pretty village situated close to the River Severn. The church had been built around 1200 from red sandstone and had a plain tiled roof with

St Michael's Church, Ford (there was no burial ground during Edward's incumbency).

some alterations having been made in the fourteenth century.[54] It also had oak-timbered beams, a fine glass window depicting the crucifixion and an ancient stone font.[55] The census of 1851 recorded the population of Ford as 341 and the parish covered 2,140 acres. Sir Offley Wakeman was Lord of the Manor and the major landowner in the area.[56]

Edward's first entry in the parish registers was a baptism which took place on 28 December 1851 carried out for the daughter of a pig dealer aptly named John Pigg of Alberbury. On this occasion he recorded himself as an 'officiating priest' and may well have been deputising at this stage and awaiting a formal appointment. The previous incumbent, John Wason, had taken up a perpetual curacy in Sheepscomb in Gloucestershire.[57] Edward had beautiful copperplate handwriting and would record the ages at which the child had been baptised and, on those occasions where he had to christen a child at home due to illness, he would note this in the registers.

His duties as vicar in this small, undemanding parish were few: only a handful of baptisms and, at most, three marriages to conduct per year. Burials took place in adjoining parishes as it would not be until July 1861 that the parish gained a consecrated burial ground.[58] Ford was part of the diocese of Hereford, and Edward's position

Page from Ford parish registers during Edward's ministry.

was further cemented when, six months after taking up his appointment,[59] he was made a surrogate for the whole diocese.[60] This meant that Edward was now authorised to stand in for his fellow clergy at such times when they needed to be away from their parish. It is unlikely that the rents from his tenants brought in a great income; after all, it had taken him three years to pay back his father's debts to Darwin and Wedgwood, but he would have had a comfortable lifestyle. Demands on Edward's time in such a small parish were modest; there was always the Sunday sermon, of course, caring for the sick, and there is evidence that he played a part in educating the local children, but he also had a good social life.

Edward was a member of the Royal British Bowmen and attended many archery meetings.[61] Archery had been a valued skill since the conquest and kings had gone to great lengths to ensure that they had enough men with the required skills. As early as the sixteenth century, societies dedicated to the bow and arrow sprang up. The Royal British Bowmen, formed in 1787, were the first society to accept women members and at York in 1844 the first Grand National Archery Meeting was held.[62] Edward and his sister Mary Louisa competed at the twelfth meeting which was held in Shrewsbury during August 1855.[63] A guinea donation allowed you to compete to win the £400 worth of prizes [over £30,000 today], gave two entrance tickets, and an invitation to the ball on the second evening when the winners were announced.[64]

The Grand National meetings were held in a different part of the country every year and attracted people from throughout the United Kingdom. Unfortunately, the meeting at Shrewsbury was hit by inclement weather which saw a vastly reduced number of visitors, with just fifty-nine ladies and eighty-six gentlemen competing. Held at the racecourse site, it was wet and, the bane of all archers, extremely windy. Edward and Mary Louisa were not deterred by the bad weather and entered the ladies and gentlemen's competitions but did not win any prizes. On the following day, the rain abated for some of the morning, but the heavens opened once again for the afternoon.[65] Edward maintained his archery skills and at the annual meeting of the North Cardiganshire Archery Club in 1865, held at Aberystwyth, he won the Gentleman's Medal.

Edward was also keen on shooting and he applied for a game licence on an annual basis.[66]

Unfortunately, as a cartoon which appeared in *Punch Magazine* seems to indicate, he was not a very good shot. The cartoon depicts Edward and a gamekeeper holding their guns as a pheasant flies close by and the caption reads:

'Mr Muckleston (after missing his Bird for the twentieth time), "I say Gaskins, I do believe the Birds are frightened at me!" Old Keeper (blandly), "They didn't ought to be, Sir!"'[67]

Edward also attended numerous other social events, on some occasions with his widowed mother and unmarried sister Mary Louisa. One of the biggest social events of the year was the annual Shropshire Hunt Ball. This was an event which the aristocracy and prominent gentry would want to be seen at and, if you were not a member of the hunt, attendance was strictly by invitation only. It was such an important event that the local newspapers would publish a list of all the attendees at the ball.[68] It was also known as the 'Bachelor Ball', due to the parade of many young ladies vying to catch the eye of the eligible bachelors in attendance. Edward first attended this event, held at the Lion Assembly Rooms, in 1846 as a twenty-six-year-old who had just obtained his first university degree. His sister and mother were to join him two years later, although he attended alone the year after that. It wasn't for a further five years and after his father's death that, in 1854, Edward would once again join the aristocracy and select and fashionable gentry at this ball, this time with his mother and sister Mary Louisa. Whether Edward was looking for a wife at this stage is not clear; he did have his widowed mother and unmarried sister to take care of any domestic-related issues and to accompany him to those events where a female partner would be expected.

The ball was be widely reported, and, describing the ball on Wednesday 16 January 1856, the reporter from *Eddowes Shrewsbury Journal* wrote:

'SHROPSHIRE HUNT BALL: This annual reunion came off, on Thursday night last, with more than ordinary éclat. The spacious music hall in which the ball took place, was tastefully decorated for the occasion, and an excellent band was supplied by our excellent townsman, Mr Walter C. Hay. The company started to arrive shortly before ten, and from that time until twelve o'clock a constant stream of arrivals furnished large accessions to the gay and brilliant party. The ball was opened about half past ten, by the Viscount Hill and the Marchioness of Stafford, followed by the Marquis of Stafford and Lady Emily Bridgeman. At one o'clock the party retired to the supper room, where a most sumptuous repast was laid out, provided by Mr Careswell, the spirited lessee of the Public Rooms. On returning to the ballroom the dancing was resumed and kept up with unabated vigour until an advanced hour in the morning.'[69]

The ball had traditionally been held in the Assembly Rooms at the Lion Hotel; this was the first year at a different venue and no doubt the lessee was keen to make a very good impression. Whether Edward, by now thirty-five years old, decided to give up attending the ball or if the invitations simply ceased arriving, we do not know, but this ball appears to have been the last he attended.

On 29 October 1853, Edward, now as a man of some importance, was a guest with his sister Mary Louisa, on the inaugural passenger steam train from Shrewsbury to Hereford. On board were the directors of the Shrewsbury and Hereford Railway Company, contractors, engineers and the nobility and gentry of Shropshire, including the local Members of Parliament. Shrewsbury's station had been built in 1848, but this was the first railway line for Hereford. It was a fine day and the steam train, consisting of two engines and fourteen passenger carriages, were brightly covered in flags and bunting. A troop of musicians also joined the train, which ensured the whole event took place with music, pomp and ceremony, and the travellers were welcomed at the stations along the way. During the 1850s the opening of new railway lines were important events worthy of great celebration. In all 250 people were on board for the two-and-a-half-hour journey. On arrival in Hereford at 2pm everyone was transported to the Shire Hall for an elegant luncheon with the Mayor of Hereford and several dignitaries of the town. The meal was followed by many congratulatory speeches before the company departed for the return journey at 6pm.[70] The railway, and especially the Great Western Railway Company, were to play an interesting part in Edward's life.

Whilst Edward was enjoying his new appointment and a varied social life, Queen Victoria was taking a personal interest in the welfare of her soldiers who were busy fighting the Crimean War. She was horrified to hear of the conditions they suffered and, as well as sending them beef tea and Windsor soup, she would regularly correspond with Florence Nightingale. The conclusion of this conflict would see her introduce the Victoria Cross, the highest award for valour.[71]

There was also the occasional issue to be dealt with relating to tenants on Edward's estates. In 1855 he made his first known court appearance when the case 'The Reverend Edward Muckleston v James Higgs' was heard in the Welshpool County Court.[72] Edward was attempting to reclaim rent for land at Pintervin, but on this occasion he was unsuccessful as, his Honour E. L. Richards felt that Edward had not presented a good enough case.[73] Edward improved his litigation skills and made full use of the legal system, so much so that at the start of a case just over three years later,[74] it was worthy of comment. He was claiming £2 [about £140 today] for damage done to some trees on his land and the reporter opened his article by writing, 'A Litigious Parson – Muckleston v Harris. The plaintiff in this case is perhaps unnecessary to describe as the Reverend E. Muckleston of Ford, for by with the frequency he appears in this court, he has obtained for himself a wide notoriety.'[75] It is unknown how many cases he had brought before the courts in this short time period, but it was clearly a number worthy of comment.

Edward employed a bailiff by the name of Edward Edwards to deal with the day-to-day running of his properties. In the case of Edwards v Peate brought to the County Court in February 1859, Edwards was suing a tenant for £12-8s-0d rent [around £750 today] alleged to be owed for a farm at Pentrewern. During this case he mentioned that he had written to Reverend Edward the landlord, in Scotland, and a letter was produced. The defendant's council stated that he felt the letter had been written especially for this case and that a true reflection of events had not been given, basically calling Edward a liar. One thing that became clear from this case was how often

Edward meddled in his bailiff's duties and Edwards had to defend his master's actions on several occasions during the hearing, repeatedly saying that Mr Muckleston had made a mistake.[76]

The fact that Edward was in Scotland may well mean that he was a regular visitor to the McKay and Munro families at Cromarty, whose family marriage he had conducted ten years earlier.

During the 1850s Edward appears to have been a popular clergyman. From June 1856, for just over a year, he acted as curate for the parish of King's Heath leaving a curate, by the name of John Breeze, to take care of things at Ford. King's Heath, now absorbed as a suburb of the city of Birmingham, was then a relatively newly created rural village and parish in Worcestershire, only appearing on maps from 1840.[77] The Anglican Church was not built until 1860 and as a result Edward conducted the services in the local schoolroom.[78] His time in this parish went well, as on his retirement from this curacy it was reported that, 'a large number of the friends of the Reverend Edward Muckleston met in the schoolrooms of the village of King's Heath'. Edward was presented with a handsome silver inkstand bearing the inscription, 'presented together with a Bible to the Rev. Edward Muckleston MA, by the poorer parishioners and a few other friends, on his retirement from the curacy of King's Heath, Worcestershire 17 September 1857'.[79] The inkstand was treasured and remained in the family until the 1970s.

By the end of 1857 Edward had returned to Ford to pick up his duties. The services of John Breeze were no longer required; however, within three years John would obtain his own permanent position as rector of nearby Hanwood.

Edward would continue to use the legal system to solve his disputes, but a conflict with a fellow clergyman, which saw him in court as a defendant, would have far-reaching consequences.

Chapter Five

The Uprooting of Reverend Muckleston

THREE MONTHS PRIOR TO LEAVING TO UNDERTAKE the curacy at King's Heath, Edward purchased a new home in Ford, which was described as, 'A superior country mansion, with about two acres of land, with ornamental pleasure grounds including a fish pond, orchard and a garden, stabling and commodious outbuildings.'[80] In 1856[81] he paid the previous owner, Thomas Harley Rough, £480 [about £33,500 today] for the property known as Ford Hall and was admitted as a tenant by the Lord of the Manor. He engaged a housekeeper, Mrs Maria Brittain, whose marriage to William Bishop he would conduct at the parish church a couple of years later.[82]

A little more than two years after purchasing Ford Hall[83] a notice appeared in the Shrewsbury newspapers advertising the sale of the contents of the house at Quarry Place, as requested by 'Captain' Muckleston's executors. The items were to be sold by auction and the newspaper listed the objects which were for sale, everything from mahogany wardrobes and carpets to wine glasses and dinner services. From the description of the sale we learn that the house

Ford Hall (circa 2012).

had seven bedchambers, the contents of which, including the beds, were to be sold. The sale was to take place over two days and although an extensive list of items appeared in the newspaper, a more detailed catalogue was available on request; this listed the items room by room and showed that the family had lived in great comfort.[84] For example, there were 164 cut glass wine glasses, twelve wine coolers and a mahogany dining table which measured eleven feet six inches by four feet six inches and had ten matching chairs allowing for limited entertaining. Edward clearly did not require the contents of this house at his new home, or maybe it was a way of raising some money. The sale may not have been a total success, as some of the contents did remain at Quarry Place and it was eventually let as a furnished property.

One of the tenants to live at Quarry Place was Captain Morse who was named in a hearing when Richard Tittensor, a local upholsterer, took Edward to court for an overdue payment. Edward was to claim that his tenant had requested some of the work which had been carried out and it was therefore his responsibility to pay the outstanding sum of £6-11s-6½d. Richard Tittensor had made several attempts to obtain payment since he had been engaged in 1857 and presented his bill to Edward for £35-11-6½d [around £2,000 today]. Two years later, on 8 April 1859, Edward paid £29 [approximately £1,700] towards the bill. Being more than patient, Richard Tittensor allowed a further three years to elapse before once again asking for payment of the outstanding amount. This is when Edward declared that the debt belonged to Captain Morse as that amount represented the work which his tenant had requested. The Captain was no longer a tenant and once written to advised that he had a receipt from Edward declaring that all monies due had been paid in full and therefore the debt was not his. Finally, almost six years after the work had been carried out, the upholsterer felt he had no recourse other than to put the situation before the courts and on Monday 2 March 1863, the case of Tittensor v Muckleston was heard at Shrewsbury County Court.[85] The judge found in favour of the upholsterer and not only did Edward have to pay the debt, but also the expenses of the legal representatives and the witnesses of both parties.[86] Yet another example of Edward not wanting to part with money until forced to do so.

Shortly after Edward had moved to Ford Hall, George Tomline sold the advowson to John Naylor for £550 [approximately £32,500 today] and he became Edward's new patron.[87] In 1860 George Tomline MP was one of the hundred eminent persons to sign a letter sent to Napoleon III, asking for help in building a channel tunnel to connect the railways of England and France. Although ownership of the advowson gave him the right to appoint the vicar, as Edward was already in post John Naylor could not remove him; he simply had the right to appoint a subsequent vicar and then only with the bishop's approval.

Conflict arose between the new patron and his incumbent just two years later. Edward employed a wheelwright by the name of Mr Trentham to make a gate and had identified some trees on his land at Ford Hall which could be cut down for this purpose; he subsequently received notice from John Naylor that he had no right to cut down these trees and his patron threatened Edward with action in the ecclesiastical court. Edward argued that the previous patron George Tomline had, in the past, allowed him to cut down trees to build sheds and he was totally unaware that he was not allowed to do so. He believed that as he owned the freehold to the land he could do as he wished with the property. It was a complicated situation, as the position of vicar of this parish did not include a vicarage; Edward had purchased his own home and as such Ford Hall was not technically glebe land as was claimed.

Edward had agreed to sell the surplus wood, not needed to make the gate, to Mr Trentham. Due to the intervention of John Naylor, and Edward erring on the side of caution, the wheelwright did not receive the full amount of timber which had been agreed and as such refused to make any payment to Edward for the wood. Once more turning to the courts,[88] Edward sued Mr Trentham for the sum of £5. Edward won this case as it was agreed that he should receive payment for the trees which had been removed, even though they were not the full number agreed to in the contract.[89]

Trees were to be Edward's downfall. He had a neighbour in Ford, a fellow clergyman by the name of Reverend R. Lingen Burton, Vicar of St Giles' Church in Shrewsbury, who had previously been Vicar of Ford,[90] and who owned an adjoining property. There were three trees on Reverend

Burton's land that were close to the fence which divided Edward's land from his. For an unknown reason, bad feeling had arisen between the two parties and on a cold morning in February 1860, Edward was observed acting suspiciously near the boundary trees by Mary Bishop, who kept a post office and school at Ford. When she had a closer look, she found soil had been removed from around the base of the three trees and there were also marks on the bark. She informed Reverend Burton and he then asked his lawyer to deal with the situation. The reverend's lawyer tried to avoid a court case by offering to allow Edward to donate to the infirmary to compensate for his poor behaviour. Edward refused this offer and as a result was taken to the petty sessions where Reverend Burton said that Edward had never raised any issue about the trees with him. The damage was found to be negligible and Edward was fined three pence for the damage and one pound three shillings costs or three weeks' imprisonment.[91] Edward paid the fine.

A couple of days after this case came to court,[92] the tenant of the land on which the trees stood was informed that there had been further damage and went to look. Edward had not been observed near the property, but there were footprints. The tenant called the local policeman, PC Pearce, who was told about the further damage and that fresh footprints had been found near the trees and that they appeared to be coming from the direction of Edward's property. The policeman took a spade and removed the footmark near a tree. PC Pearce was to testify that, on approaching Edward in Shrewsbury, the conversation went:

'Halloo Pearce is that you? I said yes it is; Is it you Mr Muckleston? He then asked me if I had been at Ford. I said yes. He said is anything the matter there? I said the three trees had been injured again. I asked him to allow me to feel the bottom of his boots. He did so and then said, "Am I suspected?" I asked if he had the same boots on then as he had on the morning before. He said yes. I asked if he would let me have his boots to see if they corresponded with the footmarks. He asked if I wanted them tonight or whether it would not do in the morning. I said I would rather have them then. I went to Ford with him. He went into the house and pulled off the boots, in my presence, and gave them to me.'[93]

PC Pearce was to compare the boots to the footmark and found that they were a match. It was stated in court that the boot was not the type a labourer would wear, and the placing of the nails and wear in the toe made it a perfect match.

The damage on this occasion was more extensive and it looked as if a billhook had been used on the trees. In court for a second time in April, Edward's defence counsel was to argue that he did not own such an implement and that he had fully co-operated with the police inquiry.[94] Ann Davies, his then-housekeeper, was called, and she gave him an alibi for the time period during which the offence could have taken place. Charles Pugh, who regularly worked for Edward, testified that there was not a billhook on Edward's premises and a shoemaker stated that the shoe was a common design. Despite this defence, Edward was found guilty and the magistrates stated that the sentence would therefore be the heaviest the law empowered them to inflict, namely 3s. damages and a fine of £5, including 25s. costs, [around £300 today] or in default, a month's imprisonment with hard labour. In addition, they made very damning comments about Edward's character saying that they 'characterised the case as one of the meanest and most disgraceful cases that had ever come before the court'.[95] Edward's lawyer stated that they planned to appeal to the quarter sessions and asked for bail several times, but this request was declined, and consequently the fine was paid.

Convicted twice, Edward's position as Perpetual Curate of Ford was starting to look untenable.

The very public dispute continued after the judgment when Reverend Burton wrote to the *Shrewsbury Chronicle*, upset at the criticism inferring that he had been harsh in dragging Edward to court. In his letter printed in the newspaper, he mentioned that he had offered to settle out of court, but this offer was turned down and Edward allegedly responded through his solicitor that he 'courted inquiry'. Reverend Burton therefore felt that having had the offer rejected once, it was unlikely to be accepted on the second occasion. He also denied any provocation which may have caused Edward to act in such a way and was not aware that the injured trees had caused any problems for his neighbour. However, he did admit there had been frequent conflict between the two clergymen since shortly after Edward's arrival in the parish.[96]

At the time this letter was published, Edward was in London but had obtained a copy of the publication, and a week later wrote to the newspaper from his lodgings in St James'. He stated that the Reverend Burton's letter was untrue from start to finish, and 'Ever since I entered the parish of Ford, he has behaved in a most hostile and determined manner against me directly and indirectly' and 'his conduct towards me, for now eight years, has been most offensive and unneighbourly, and most unbecoming of a man of honour'. Edward felt that had he been before the county court, instead of in front of the magistrates, he would have had a better outcome, as he would have been able to state his case under oath and had a jury to decide his guilt or innocence.[97] He would have almost certainly have had to swear an oath in front of the magistrates and it therefore appears that he was being rather disingenuous.

Many of the parishioners of Ford were highly entertained by the behaviour of the two reverend gentlemen, but others were not. Minutes entered in the churchwarden's account book record a meeting of the ratepayers of the parish which took place shortly before the second trial.[98] It had been called by Thomas Hudson, a thirty-two-year-old farmer, and the minutes indicate that the churchwarden had been requested to ask Edward for the keys to the church but had been refused them. They also required access to the vestry, where apparently Edward had placed some benches and books which had been taken from the school. The reason for the removal of the school equipment was possibly only known to Edward. It was proposed by Mr Hudson and seconded by Edward Bufton, the fifty-six-year-old local grocer and druggist, that the churchwarden, Edward Hall, should demand the benches and books from Edward and, should he refuse to hand over the items, to give notice so that a further meeting should be arranged. There were just over forty ratepayers in the township, from a population of around 350, but only three individuals plus the churchwarden had signed the minutes; it is therefore not clear exactly how many people attended the meeting. Besides Hudson, Bufton and Hall, the only other signature was for David Evans, a farmer and the tenant of Reverend Burton's property. All the signatories, except for the churchwarden, were to give evidence against Edward in the ensuing court case.

Almost five weeks later, the minutes record a further meeting, called of all the parishioners, in the vestry room,[99] suggesting that they had obtained the keys to the church. This meeting was rearranged to the following day at five o'clock in the afternoon, due to the non-attendance of the churchwarden at the first meeting. The second meeting duly took place, and, on this occasion, it was proposed by Mr Bufton, and seconded by Mr David Evans, that the chairman, Thomas Hudson, should write to John Allen, the Archdeacon of Shropshire, 'to know how we are to act as regards the conduct of the Rev. Ed. Muckleston'. The minutes were written upside down at the back of the account book but do not detail the names or number of attendees. Was it just a small handful of individuals who were possibly siding with Reverend Burton and wanted to remove Edward from his position as vicar, or was the whole parish embarrassed by their clergyman's actions? In general, he appears to have been very popular with the poorer parishioners in his previous posts and there is no reason to believe this had not been the case in Ford.

Whether through defiance or total ignorance as to what was afoot, Edward had returned to the parish and, on Monday 4 June, baptised James Bates, the one-year-old son of the postman Richard Bates and his wife Mary. Reverend John Breeze had stood in for him during May and it was

Edward's first entry in the parish registers since the trials had taken place.

This baptism was to be Edward's last in the parish. No doubt the letter had been sent to the archdeacon and Edward was called to a meeting with the Bishop of Hereford, Renn Hampden Dickson. No record survives of what was said during this meeting, if one was even made, but on 3 July Edward sat before Richard Johnson, a gentleman and notary public, who drew up and acted as an impartial witness to non-contentious documents. Edward was resigning as Perpetual Curate of Ford and in the document stated that he is relocating and as such can no longer carry on his duties in that parish. He goes on to say that he is not being 'compelled thereto by force fear fraud or any other sinister design' and that he is leaving of his free will and waivers all rights which went with the position. He appointed Thomas Evans a gentleman of Hereford and John Burder of Westminster to act on his behalf in relation to the benefice and signed the document with Mr Johnson, his clerk and accountant acting as witnesses. The document was sent to the bishop and on 18 July 1860 Renn Dickson formerly accepted his resignation.[100]

Only a bishop had the power to remove a perpetual curate from his post and the alternative to his resignation would have been to take Edward to task through the ecclesiastical courts. I suspect that at their meeting Renn Dickson advised Edward on his best course of action and, knowing Edward's nature, ensured that everything was tied up legally and that there would be no further claims relating to his position at Ford.

Edward had been popular in King's Heath, where he had acted as curate for a year, and it is not surprising that in the same month, despite his resignation, he should have been invited to the consecration of the new church, dedicated to All Saints, in his old parish. The ceremony was carried out by the newly appointed Henry Philpott, Bishop of Worcester, whom Edward would one day serve under.[101]

Edward's former curate, the Vicar of Hanwood, John Breeze, then acted as surrogate for the parish of Ford until the next vicar, the Reverend John Wingfield, took up his duties in October 1860.

Edward let out his imposing home in Ford to his brother-in-law, William Lyon, at a very attractive rent. William had previously been living in Llanyblodwell, some eighteen miles distant. Quarry Place also being rented out, Edward may have made it a provision that his widowed mother and unmarried sister remain at Ford. The 1861 census records William, his wife, two daughters, sister-in-law and mother-in-law, all residing at Ford Hall along with a governess, cook, lady's maid, housemaid and a footman.

Despite swearing on oath that his reason for stepping down from his position was the fact that he was moving to a new permanent residence, Edward would spend the next five years moving from place to place.

Chapter Six

The Itinerant Years

FOR THE NEXT FEW YEARS, EDWARD, NOW FORTY-one years old, would live a rather itinerant existence. He was probably too embarrassed to spend much time at Ford and Quarry Place had a tenant. He had his estates to care for; however he employed a bailiff and left much of the basic work to him, but he did take an interest in situations which may impact on his properties and lands. One such situation was the proposal made by the Mayor and Aldermen of Shrewsbury for a new general market.[102] The plan was to create a new area for the market in the part of the town known as Mardol and Shoplatch, and it was proposed that an area of 5,000 to 6,000 square yards would be required. Edward made it known that he would be happy to sell his properties in the area to make way for the market.[103] A market stands on this site today.

Edward's entry on the 1861 census shows that he was visiting David Thomas, a farmer, and his family in Llanfyllin, Montgomeryshire, Wales, and his occupation is recorded as, 'Clergyman without cure of souls'. Despite coming from a landed gentry background, and many in his position would have recorded themselves as a 'landed proprietor', it is obvious that Edward still saw his position as a clergyman as the main role in his life.

A year after leaving Ford, he wrote from Warwick to Mary Rees, one of his tenants, as he needed to return to Shropshire for a short time:

Warwick, July 1st 1861,

Dear Mrs Rees,

Can I sleep at your house on Wednesday night, the 10th? As I shall have to be at a magistrates meeting on the 10th I shall not arrive at your house till the evening. If you say 'Yes' as I hope you will, please to buy for my dinner a duck and a fowl, and pay for it, and I will repay you again. I shall leave your house on Thursday for Salop, and thence to London again. I come down now on purpose to face that wicked old man James Price, before the magistrates. I shall return to London on Friday morning. I hope the change of air has done Mrs E. Wall and baby good. I trust your hay harvest is going on well. Here everybody is busy on it. I saw them carrying it today, and such crops of hay, beans, peas, oats and corn I never saw before. One line to me would be very satisfactory to me. Pleased to have washed my nightshirt, and the other dirty things, if you have time by Tuesday night. I do not think I shall come to your house till six or seven o'clock. Pleased to get my night shirt repaired in the neck and in the back; it is torn or a hole is in it. Believe me, your obliged,

Edward Muckleston.

In a further letter he also asked for ale to be brewed for his tenants. Mary Rees had been a tenant of Edward's for eight years and he had first stayed with her a year earlier and on several subsequent occasions. Edward had contacted her towards the end of 1859 looking for lodgings to use when he needed to visit the area and Mary's daughter had written back saying that she was happy to have him to stay.

The relationship between landlord and tenant would ultimately break down. Edward accepted the hospitality she gave but failed to pay the bills associated with his visits. Things came to a head nine months after the visit referred to in the letter,[104] when Edward told Mary Rees she had to leave the house at once. She had requested a proper receipt for her rent, and he refused to give her one unless she gave him a note to say that he owed her nothing. Mary did not leave her home and the matter was dropped until, in a most unchristian act on Christmas Day 1862, Edward gave her notice to quit her property on Lady Day next, which was the 25 March 1863.[105] The loss of her home spurred Mary Rees to take Edward to court. They both appeared before the magistrates in October 1863 when Mary was claiming £13-11s-6d [over £800 today] from her former landlord, which was the equivalent of seventy days' wages for a skilled labourer or a year's wages for a live-in servant, and would have been a significant amount of money to her.[106] She supplied copies of the unpaid bills for board and other items requested by Edward, plus a copy of the above letter; however, the magistrates decided that there was no evidence that a contract had been entered into and she lost her case. Edward testified that he believed she was allowing him to stay with her out of courtesy.[107]

Although he had resigned, his problems at Ford had been widely reported and Edward would have found it difficult to get work within the Church. He would subsequently advise those collating the Clergy Lists that between 1860 and 1865 he held the position of Curate of Warsop, a parish near Mansfield in Nottinghamshire. Situated on the outskirts of Sherwood Forest, the Reverend Philip Dawson Bland was the rector and all evidence points to Edward's involvement in Warsop's parish affairs being minimal. There is no trace of Edward's name in the churchwarden accounts or vestry minutes. He undertook very few baptisms, officiated on no marriages and just two consecutive burials on 6 and 17 August 1862. Reverend Bland carried out most of the church activity in Warsop and it is likely that Edward simply covered the parish for very short periods when the incumbent had business elsewhere and then not beyond the summer of 1862.

In October 1861 Edward joined his mother and sister at Llandudno in North Wales. Elizabeth and Mary Louisa had been staying at the seaside town since August and

Llandudno from the Parade, 1860.

whilst the ladies' usual abode was listed as Ford in Shropshire, Edward's was given as Edwinstowe Rectory.[108] Edwinstowe was a large village in Sherwood Forest around four and a half miles from Warsop, where legend had it that Robin Hood married Maid Marion in the church. The Reverend William Hayward Ibotson MA was the long-standing Vicar of Edwinstowe. Whether Edward was staying with Reverend Ibotson or was acting as curate for him is not clear and Edward may well have been assisting in various parishes in the Mansfield area on an 'as-required' basis. Edward's assertion that he had been working in Warsop for a five-year period does appear to have been an exaggeration; his intention may have been to make it look as if he had continuous employment when, in reality, little more than a year was spent working in Nottinghamshire.

Following his visit to Llandudno in November 1861, he was once again on the move and was recorded as attending the Anglesey Hunt[109] and a few days before Christmas, that same year, he was staying at the Queens Hotel in Cheltenham.[110] It would have been here that he would have heard about the death of Prince Albert, Queen Victoria's beloved husband of twenty-one years, at the young age of forty-two. His death was recorded as being due to typhoid fever. Victoria was left with nine fatherless children aged four to twenty-one years old and was thrown into deep mourning.

Around this time Edward was living at Llanfechan near Oswestry and had travelled from Warwick to Paddington to attend the Cattle Show.[111] On the return journey a porter had put him into a second-class carriage near the engine, along with seven other passengers. Edward claimed that the train had hardly gone a mile before he felt a jerking motion of the springs and that he was tossed around. He put his head out of the window and spoke to the engine driver, who reassured him that he was in no danger and that there was no need to stop until the train arrived in Reading. Edward was to later say that he could not stay in his seat as he was tossing around so badly and, on arrival at Reading, he left the train.[112]

The case of Muckleston v The Great Western Railway was heard in Reading on 7 May 1862, with Edward claiming £1-2s-0d [about £65 today] from the railway company, being 12s-6d expenses incurred at the Great Western Hotel and 9s-6d for the railway fare from Reading to Warwick. He explained to the court that after forty miles of being tossed around he felt too sick to continue the journey and spent the night at the hotel to enable him to recover and had continued his journey the next morning. Edward had written to Mr Kelley, the superintendent for the railway, asking for a refund of the expenses, but was told that he could not entertain it. Judge John F. Fraser Esq questioned Edward asking if he had requested to be put into another carriage when they reached Reading, but Edward said that, due to the severity of his headache, he had not as he could not have continued the journey. Edward did admit that the offer of another carriage was made, that the springs were examined, and he had been informed that they were not broken.

Mr Slocombe, acting for the railway company, asked Edward if there was a good deal of 'chaffing' from the other passengers within the carriage regarding his fears. Edward stated that they were also frightened, eliciting a great deal of laughter from those in court, but Edward continued to insist that he was no more frightened than they were.

Edward was asked if he could eat when he reached Reading and he confirmed that he had some tea. The judge observed that Edward was claiming 12s-6d [around £37 today] expenses at the hotel and went on to say that he had also stayed at the hotel last evening, had eaten dinner, not tea, and it had cost 9s [approximately £26 today], not including servants. He commented that Edward's stomach could therefore not have been that delicate, which elicited even more laughter from the people in court. Edward was asked if he had applied to use his excursion ticket on the train that he caught the next day, but he claimed to have been advised that it was not transferable.

Witnesses were called for the railway company. The inspector at Reading station was to say that no complaint had been made to him. The porter and guard on the train testified that the carriages were designed to hold twelve people and that the train was not overcrowded; when Edward had asked to leave the train at Reading and he opened the door, there was some larking in the carriage. He also said that he did not notice if Edward was pale or not and that the carriage in which he sat did not oscillate more than others; however, having sat in a rear carriage himself, the judge disputed this.

In passing judgment, the judge said that he had to dismiss the claim, otherwise everyone who undertook a train journey and who was jolted slightly would be looking to have a good dinner at the railway company's expense and then he could also see claims coming in against the Steam Navigation Company for sea sickness. Once again, a great deal of laughter was heard throughout the court. The Great Western Railway Company asked for costs and the judge granted these. This was an embarrassing

International Exhibition at Kensington in 1862.

situation for Edward and one which was to engender a great deal of ill will between him and the Great Western Railway Company (GWR).

A month after Edward took the GWR to court,[113] in June 1862, the International Exhibition took place at Kensington. Attracting over six million visitors, there were over 28,000 exhibitors from thirty-six countries, and it would last for six months.[114] The seventy-year-old MP Robert Aglionby Slaney, the husband of Edward's cousin Elizabeth, had an accident at the opening, fell through the floor and died from gangrene a couple of weeks later.[115] Edward exhibited a specimen of hard building stone at this event. The stone had been taken from Whitsburne Quarry at Leigh, one of Edward's many business ventures. Leigh was situated not far from Worthen where he owned several properties. Near to Edward's exhibit was one from a Mr S. Peake, who was the proprietor of Berwig Quarry, Minera near Wrexham, who was also exhibiting some building stones.[116] Mr Peake and Edward were to form a partnership and purchased a lead mine at Pontblyddyn near Mold in Clwyd.[117] Lead was in great demand due to the industrial revolution, but this was a decision that Edward would ultimately regret.

Edward continued his interest in archery and membership of the British Bowmen, and he attended the Grand National Archery meeting, which in 1862 took place in Worcester. The backdrop was once again the River Severn and the event was catered by the landlord of the Crown Hotel. Edward watched the archery and attended the ball which followed the event.[118]

The following year Edward officiated at a wedding[119] when, on this occasion, he conducted the marriage of Mr William Lucas of Corfe Castle and Miss Sarah Sly of Bindon Abbey. The wedding took place at Wool Church in Dorset which was close to the bride's residence. He was assisted in conducting the ceremony by the Reverend Bracebridge Hall.[120] William Lucas was a thirty-six-year-old miller born in Dorset and Sarah Sly was the twenty-six-year-old niece of another local miller, John Sly, who was quite well-to-do, farming 210 acres and employing twelve men. As with the wedding he officiated at in Scotland, I have been unable to find a connection between the Muckleston family and those of the happy couple.

A few days later Edward received an invitation to a Yeomanry Ball which was taking place thirty-five miles to the north-east of Dorset, in Salisbury on 5 June 1863. Held at the Royal Hotel Assembly Rooms, it was being hosted by the officers of the Yeomanry Cavalry, suggesting that Edward had kept his father's army links and he decided to attend.[121] By now Edward had returned to giving his address as Ford Hall, although the Shropshire Directory for this year gave his address as Hope, which was very close to his properties in Worthen.[122]

Little is known of Edward's activities over the next twelve months or so, but in November 1864, while he was living at Greenfields Cottage in Minsterley Shropshire, he is known to have purchased some ironmongery in Shrewsbury. As one of his employees was travelling on the 3.30pm train, he had requested for his purchase to be taken to the train for Evans, his servant, to bring to him. Evans had been told that if there was anything to pay, he should pay it. An employee of the ironmongers did take the bag of items to the train and met a police constable called Williams who was in the employ of the London and North Western Railway Company. The ironmonger's assistant asked Williams what he should do with the items and was advised to take it to the platform from where the train started. Evans duly arrived back without the parcel and when asked, Williams the policeman stated that he had put the bag in the van of an evening train to Ministerley. This caused Edward some inconvenience, as he had to send someone to collect them.

Edward had decided to try his hand at brickmaking, and he employed several men to build an oven for him. He purchased some iron bars in Wrexham to place in the oven and arranged for them to be transported from Wrexham to Ministerley by the London and North Western Railway Company. On 10 June 1865 Edward called at Ministerley railway station, paid for the carriage of the bars and was informed they had arrived two days earlier. He duly sent a carter to collect them on 13 June, but he returned without them having been told they had yet to be paid for. The next day Edward sent the carter once again but, on this occasion, he returned with just four bars. About a week later Edward was told that they could have them as they had 'found them to be paid for'. It was three weeks before Edward had ownership of all the bars and consequently, during this time, he could not burn any bricks. The 4,000 bricks which were ready for burning were ruined by rain due to the delay. Once again Edward felt that the London and North Western railway company had caused him expense and inconvenience, and he wrote to them requesting compensation but was unsuccessful with his claim.

This was the second time Edward had been caused difficulty by this railway company and he decided to take them to court. The two cases of Muckleston v The London and North Western Railway Company were eventually heard in the Bloomsbury County Court some eighteen months later.[123] In his first case he was claiming £8 compensation [about £485 today] for the delay in receiving the thirty-two iron bars. He brought a large number of witnesses to the London court to support his case. His carters confirmed several visits to the station attempting to obtain the bars, but each time was turned away due to non-payment. His brickmaker confirmed he was paid thirty shillings a week, that the four men under him received fifteen shillings and that they were all idle for three weeks awaiting the iron. Edward was claiming the cost of the men's wages, plus the cost of constantly sending to the station for the bars.

The railway company was to say they did not release the bars until they had been paid for and on the first visits no payment had been made. A letter was produced, written by Edward to the railway company regarding the incident, but the contents disagreed with what was said in court and Edward tried to explain this away by saying that at the time of writing the letter he was receiving conflicting information from his servants as to what was happening. Each of the carters denied telling different stories to Edward and stated that the evidence they had given in court was the same as they had told him at the time. The solicitor for the railway company stated that Edward's evidence lacked credibility and, on confirming that Edward did not have a ministry in Shropshire at the time of the incident and trying to discredit his testimony, asked, 'Was there not some little unpleasantness with the Bishop?' Edward retorted that had nothing to do with the case and the judge did not allow the point the solicitor was trying to make to go any further. Edward lost this claim and the railway company was awarded costs, a very expensive case for him to lose, considering what it would have cost to bring his witnesses to the London court.[124]

Making the most of his visit, Edward's second case was in relation to the delayed ironmongery two years earlier,[125] for which he held the same railway company responsible. Once again, the judge dismissed the case, and, as on the previous occasion, Edward had to pay costs.[126] Edward's actions against railway companies were proving fruitless and expensive.

Edward continued to make great use of the railways as he travelled around the country. He had worked out that if he purchased an excursion ticket, he could leave the train at any point along the journey without being required to give up the ticket, as it was assumed that the journey was still to be completed. Perhaps looking to obtain some recompense for earlier losses or possibly just to save money, Edward then took to purchasing a ticket which covered a route one stop beyond and one stop before his required journey. Having purchased a ticket, he was to use it several times for the same trip but was subsequently caught early in March 1865. He was warned about his behaviour and avoided court by offering to make a payment of £5 [around £300 today] to the Shropshire Infirmary.

Early in this period of upheaval, Edward had worked hard to obtain another permanent position within the Church and his patience was rewarded on the death of the Reverend W. T. Hadow, the Rector of Haseley in Warwickshire, on 20 July 1865, aged sixty-nine. A new chapter was about to open in Edward's life.

Chapter Seven

A New Benefice

IN THE FIVE YEARS SINCE HE HAD LEFT FORD, EDWARD had spent some time in Warwickshire. It was here he became acquainted with a Mr Edwards-Wood, who, with a partner, was a coal master of the Tame Valley and Kingsbury collieries. In 1859 Mr Edwards-Wood purchased the advowson or patronage of the parish of Haseley, in the same county, for the price of £2,800 [over £165,000 today].

In the eleventh and twelfth centuries, Lords of the Manor built parish churches on their land and devoted farmland for the benefit of providing a parish priest with an income. As the Church also received tithes from those living in the parish, it was a way of ensuring that the estate benefitted from the tithe income. As he had surrendered land to the benefit of the Church, the Lords of the Manor insisted that they retained the right to appoint the parish priest, someone who would preach in a manner he felt fitting, would look after the morality of the tenants and it was also a way of looking after a favoured servant or a younger son by giving them a living in the Church. This became known as a patronage or an advowson, ownership of which was greatly valued. During the reformation and the dissolution of the monasteries in the sixteenth century, many of these advowsons fell into the hands of laypeople. In 1603 there were 3,849 livings in the hands of lay men out of a total of 9,284. Where the Lord of the Manor or patron was a Roman Catholic, the advowsons were removed from them and handed over to Oxford and Cambridge universities, dependant on where they were situated in the country, giving the universities the right to appoint the priest. The nomination made by the owner of the advowson was to be put before the bishop, who would generally approve the appointment.

HASELEY RECTORY.

NEXT PRESENTATION.

TO BE SOLD,

THE next PRESENTATION to the PARISH CHURCH and RECTORY of HASELEY, in the County of Warwick. The Tithes of the Parish are commuted at the annual sum of Two Hundred and Thirty-five Pounds Eighteen Shillings, which has been confirmed under the Commutation Act for England and Wales. There are also Sixty-seven Acres, Three Roods and Eleven Perches of first-rate GLEBE LAND, worth One Hundred and Fifty Pounds per annum; also a recently-erected and most commodious PARSONAGE HOUSE, with Stables, Coach Houses, and other Outbuildings, of the yearly value of Seventy-five Pounds, situated close to the Church. The present Incumbent's age—fifty-nine. The Population only two hundred and thirty-eight.

Haseley should be seen to be properly appreciated, it is beautifully situated, on a dry soil, three miles from the County Town of Warwick, on the Birmingham Turnpike Road, five miles from Leamington Spa, three miles from Kenilworth, and one mile from the "Hatton Station," on the London, Oxford, and Birmingham Great Western Railway.

Apply to Messrs. BURTON & SON, Solicitors, Daventry, or to W. EDWARDS-WOOD, Esq., Warwick, Patron of the Advowson.

Copy of the advertisement relating to the sale of the presentation rights.

Mr Edwards-Wood fell into financial difficulties; Edward loaned him £3,500 and went about raising money for him from others, but this was not enough to solve his problems. As the advowson was an asset, which he could sell but really did not want to go to that length, he decided to sell the right to appoint the next incumbent.

On paper the purchaser of the right to appoint the next vicar was William Lyon, Edward's brother-in-law, who paid £2,500 [about £150,000 today], only a few hundred pounds less than Mr Edwards-Wood had paid for the full rights. On signing the contract, the sum of £1,400 [around £83,000 today] was paid and the balance was cleared the following year. It was a great expense and risky, as it could have been some considerable time before the position became vacant. It later became clear that the purchaser was Edward himself, but he may have thought it prudent to put the rights in his brother-in-law's name to avoid questions over appointing himself. The purchase was made a year after Edward had left Ford, and he therefore knew he had a future position in the Church and just had to wait for sixty-four-year-old Reverend Hadow to either resign or pass away.

Still in financial difficulties Mr Edwards-Wood then raised a loan of £1,000 from a Mr Halford using the deeds to the advowson as security. When accused of fraudulent activity in an article in the *Staffordshire Advertiser*, by raising a mortgage on something he had sold, he wrote a letter to the newspaper, explaining, 'Everyone conversant with ecclesiastical property will know that the sale of a next presentation does not divest the patron of the advowson over which he retains a power to sell or mortgage, subject to his prior dealings therewith.'[127] This splitting of the benefits of the advowson would subsequently cause difficulties.

In 1864 Edwards-Wood and his partner applied to be declared bankrupt; fortunately for Edward, although still a significant amount, only £600 [about £35,000 today] of the loan he had made to him remained unpaid. At the bankruptcy court, as well as claiming for the debt, Edward presented an IOU for £75 for kindness received. When questioned what the debt was for, Mr Edwards-Wood explained that Edward had done him many favours: assisting him in raising loans, sometimes going as far as London to raise money and occasionally paying a commission to those prepared to make a loan. Edwards-Wood had written the IOU using the words 'kindness received' as a delicacy towards Edward. In other words, Edward had been paying what today would be termed 'backhanders' in exchange for the loans and Edwards-Wood did not want to write this on the IOU. The court asked if Edward had a living at the time and was told no, but that he had purchased the Haseley living from Edwards-Wood. The claim for £75 was declined on the grounds that they would have Protestant clergymen denounced for receiving money for kindness received.[128]

It took three years for Mr Edwards-Wood to be declared bankrupt and the mortgage of the advowson then fell to Charles and Thomas Halford. By 1870 a widow by the name of Elizabeth Brooks was the legal owner of the advowson which had passed to her husband as an inheritance from the Halfords and then to her on his death. Elizabeth Brooks and her children would spend many years contesting Edward's right to be the incumbent of Haseley, going as far as to involve the various bishops of the diocese in the dispute. Copies of deeds were supplied by numerous solicitors, but Edward also had deeds and was able to continue to assert his right to remain in the post. Mrs Brooks' argument was that the right to present the next vicar should not have been split from the advowson in the first place. To Edward's benefit was the fact that he, or his brother-in-law, had purchased the right to appoint prior to the mortgage being taken out and that at the time of his appointment, no legal challenge had been made. When Mrs Brooks died in 1896, she left the advowson to her children, who took up the fight but simply used the old arguments and had no more success than their mother.[129]

Edward was, however, in a difficult position, as he occasionally needed her permission to carry out work on the land. On 3 March 1879 he wrote:

Dear Mrs Brooks

I cannot for the life of me let the glebe land. I have offered to lower the rent but still nobody will take it. I have only one chance left and that is to build a suitable farmhouse on it. I have been offered by a tenant a reasonable rent for it if it had a farmhouse for it. I have made arrangements to build but before I do I must have your approval and signature. I have got the Bishop's. I will send you the plans for your approval. I do hope you will not refuse as you see if you do I shall not be able to let the land and consequently have no means of living as my income is derived from the rents. Times are dreadful with land especially church property. I really begin to think that England is going down fast in her land value. I hope this will find you quite well and your family. Please to reply as soon as you conveniently can.

    Believe me

Yours faithfully

Edw. Muckleston.

After all the ill feeling, you can only wonder at Mrs Brooks' reaction to this letter, but she was certainly in no hurry to reply as, on 12 March, Edward was chasing her for a response. He had applied for a land improvement loan of £510 [around £34,000 today] to build the farmhouse and had obtained permission from the bishop and William Lyon, his patron, but was then advised that the application also needed the signature of the owner of the advowson. Whether he ever received her permission is unknown, but as there are no references to a farmhouse ever being erected on Haseley glebe land, I suspect that she refused his request.

In 1891 there was a strange incident. It transpired that Edward had contacted several solicitors throughout the country trying to source a loan against the value of the advowson. A Birmingham solicitor, Mr Alfred Milward, visited Edward at his home[130] and on looking through the paperwork identified that he had not purchased the full advowson but the equity of redemption as it was subject to an old mortgage of £2,000. Edward had written to Mr Milward asking if he could source him a loan, saying that he had just bought the advowson for £4,000 [over a quarter of a million pounds today] but had needed to borrow £800 [about £50,000 today] towards the purchase from Messrs Clark of Shrewsbury who now wanted repaying.

Subsequently Alfred Milward took Edward to court for non-payment of professional services. In court, Edward's defence was that he had never engaged Mr Milward to carry out any work for him. He agreed that they had dined together on a Saturday where the matter was discussed, but he saw it as nothing more than friendly advice. When pressed if he owned the advowson, Edward said that he did but had only paid £70 [about £4,500 today] and £70 was still owing. When asked why Mr Milward was under the impression Edward had paid £4,000, Edward simply replied that was a mistake. The solicitor felt he had been deliberately misled into doing the work by Edward's misrepresentations. Edward entered a counterclaim stating that Mr Milward had kept hold of the deeds and he was therefore unable to progress any other attempts to raise the money. The judge stated that there was no formal agreement of Edward engaging the solicitor but that he would allow Mr Milward to claim for the work he did on an insurance policy. He dismissed Edward's counterclaim.[131] The deeds in question may have been those held by William Lyon, who had died in 1880 and which had passed to his wife Elizabeth, Edward's sister, although these were now valueless as it only conferred the right to appoint the next rector which had been used at Edward's appointment.

The claim by Edward about owning the advowson was almost certainly a fraudulent one, as the Brooks family retained ownership and never gave up the fight and, as new bishops were appointed, they took up their case with each new incumbent. Documents show that in January 1908 a caveat was served on the bishop against the institution of 'the present Rector of Haseley'. The case of Brooks v Muckleston even came to court in July 1909 when Edward was ninety years old. One solicitor was to observe that 'the situation is complicated and troublesome'.[132]

Try as they might, Edward would remain in post until the end of his life. Edward had been appointed in 1865 by his brother-in-law, having left his previous permanent position at Ford five years earlier, and would spend the next forty-eight years in a small but pretty parish.

Chapter Eight

Haseley

W HATEVER THE SITUATION REGARDING THE advowson, Edward's new home for the next forty-eight years would be the rectory at Haseley. It was a desirable and imposing fourteen-roomed residence filled with oak furniture, having large windows to let in the light and lots of fireplaces to keep the building warm in the cold, harsh winters. The original building had been built in the seventeenth century, but by the time of Edward's occupation it had been greatly modernised, only a small part of a barn retaining any of that century's features.

Standing outside the rectory, which was situated at the southern end of the parish facing the small, narrow, dusty track known as Firs Lane, all Edward could see were fields and the occasional farm building. There was no village, as such, and his parishioners, who numbered 224 in 1871, lived on scattered farms and smallholdings within the long ancient parish of around 1,200 acres. The settlement of Haseley had been mentioned in the Domesday Book and could be found between the parishes of Hatton and Honiley in Warwickshire. His new home stood on what

The rectory at Haseley in the early 1900s with the Reverend Edward Muckleston MA standing outside.

is said to be the highest tableland in England; the step of the hall door of the rectory being on a level with the lead roof of the high church in Warwick, the nearest large town which was some three and a half miles to the south-east.[133] The farmers grew crops of wheat, barley, oats, beans, swedes, mangolds and potatoes, as well as keeping livestock consisting mainly of cows, sheep, pigs and chickens. Being accustomed to rural life from his time at Ford, as well as spending his childhood at Bicton, the smell of manure being spread for the crops and the sound of cattle lowing as they were being taken for milking were all familiar to him.

If he turned to the right and headed southwards down the lane, leaving behind the healthier air and peacefulness of the countryside, less than a quarter of a mile from his home was the main Warwick to Birmingham road running alongside the busy Birmingham canal which had been built in 1799. This waterway had been a busy highway since the advent of the industrial revolution and was widely used for the transportation of goods.

The Falcon Inn could be found here, a hostelry where the meetings of the rector and churchwardens would take place, the church having no vestry. These premises abutted Edward's extensive garden and, when there was a change of landlord at the inn in 1877, Edward would find it necessary to consult the magistrates regarding what action he could take regarding a skittle alley built close to his fence. His concerns related to broken fences, profanities being heard and illegal gambling taking place. On the main road was Hatton Railway Station belonging to the Great Western Railway, which had been built in 1852 and was just a ten-minute walk from the rectory. This allowed Edward and the parishioners to travel north to the city of Birmingham and, due to a triangular junction completed in 1860, south to the towns of Warwick and Stratford-upon-Avon.[134]

St Mary's Church at Haseley.

If Edward turned to the left of the rectory heading north, after just a few dozen steps he came to the ancient church dedicated to St Mary surrounded by a beautiful iron fence, said to be made to the same pattern as that surrounding Buckingham Palace. This is where Edward would preach his sermons and carry out his parishioners' baptisms, marriages and funerals. It was one of Warwickshire's smallest parish churches with the nave and its barrel-vaulted roof divided by moulded oak ribs, dating back to the twelfth century and the chancel to the thirteenth century. The chancel contained the tomb of Clement Throckmorton, who died in 1573, and his wife Katherine Neville. The octagonal font dated from the fifteenth century and the high pews mostly from the eighteenth century.[135] The west tower, also added in the fifteenth century, contained three bells. There were occasions when the building had to be closed to facilitate work, such as in 1868 when Edward arranged for the chancel to be extended at a cost of £60 [around £4,000 today].

Continuing along Firs Lane about 300 yards north-east of the church, on the opposite side of the lane, could be found the lands of the Lord of the Manor, Frederick Hewlett. The Old Manor House, which this gentleman called home, was built in 1561 by Clement Throckmorton, whose initials and those of his wife appeared on the porch. The house stood in a beautiful park which contained a wide range of trees including oak, hazel, birch and ash. This park is believed to have been created by Sir Thomas de Cherlecote in 1267 or possibly his father Thomas.[136] Frederick Hewlett would build a new house not far from the old manor and eventually become the peoples' churchwarden for St Mary's Church working alongside Edward.

Interior of St Mary's Church.

Opposite the Lord of the Manor's lands, on the west side of the lane and a quarter of a mile north of the rectory, stood Haseley Glebe Farm with its timber-framed farm buildings but no farmhouse and this formed part of Edward's benefice. Glebe farms were used to support the parish priests and the incumbent could either rent them out for an income or farm them themselves. Edward initially chose to rent out the farm, but in later life he would achieve a level of fame from farming the land himself, having a great deal of success with a new crop. Although only valid as long as he was rector, ownership of this farm made Edward one of the major landowners in the area, as were Frederick Hewlett, Colin Campbell, Mr S. Burbury, and Miss M. E. Trafford Southwell, a great philanthropist who owned land and property all over the country.[137]

Near to Glebe Farm, 500 yards north of the church, stood a watermill fed by a small clear rivulet called Inchford Brook that ran through the parish. The water supply from Haseley would eventually be used to supply the town of Warwick and these new waterworks would result in a lengthy conflict between Edward and the Warwick Corporation.

Heading to the far north of his new parish past many small farms, he would find another imposing mansion, Haseley Hall. In 1891 the eminent physician Sir James Sawyer took up residence at the hall and he became a good friend to Edward, who went on to elect him vicar's churchwarden.

The church and the parish were small, and this allowed Edward time to manage his other landowning interests. The curate of nearby Hatton initially undertook the necessary functions within the church and Edward's first recorded ceremony at Haseley was the burial on 9 November 1865 of twenty-year-old Thomas Harwood. The curate continued to support the parish, but Edward returned in time to undertake his first baptism on 28 March 1866, and a marriage of a butler and lady's maid, three months later, on 26 June. From that point on, with just the odd exception, Edward conducted most of the ceremonies himself. One interesting register entry occurs on 25 September 1881 when Reverend Fred Thomas Swinburne DD, the Vicar of Acock's Green, Warwickshire appears as he conducted several baptisms for older children, aged four and above, the sons and daughters of local labourers. This visit by Reverend Swinburne was possibly at the request of some of the parishioners, as Edward had not proven popular with some of his new flock and they may not have wanted Edward to carry out their children's baptisms.

As he had done at Ford, Edward kept meticulous parish registers. When babies were privately baptised at home shortly after birth, usually due to the fear that they were about to die, he recorded this fact. When the new burial ground opened, against the entry for eight-month-old Henry Britten on 6 December 1887, he noted that this was the first Christian internment in the new burial ground. On occasions he also entered more information than was strictly required, such as this entry from 1898 where he detailed how one of his parishioners was killed. 'Charles Gamage killed at Stank Hill by being run over by the Wagon of Mr Horne of Honiley on Sunday, 29 November 1898.'

There had been some controversy over the new burial ground. In 1885 Edward had written to the Home Office regarding the fact that the existing site was almost full. An inspector made a visit to Haseley and suggested that a piece of land between the current burial ground and the rectory be used as an extension. Edward objected to this on the basis that it was too close to his home and suggested that a new burial ground should be paid for by the ratepayers. The Home Office inspector disagreed with Edward's suggestion, as farming was in a difficult state at the time and he said it was unfair to put any additional burden on the parishioners.

Two years later, on 7 February 1887, Mr Abraham Ball, the people's churchwarden for the parish at that time, called a meeting at the Falcon Inn to decide what to do, as the current burial ground had been closed due to it being full. Mr Hewlett proposed that three acres of the Featherstone charity land adjoining his property be sold to him and that one third of an acre of his land next to the churchyard would be donated for the purpose of a new burial ground. The Featherstone charity was run by trustees and the bequest of the land had been made to cover the cost of repairs to the church and roads or relief of the poor at the trustee's discretion. Prior to 1887

Mr Hewlett had been the rector's churchwarden and had regularly funded repairs to the church at his own expense as the congregation was said to be small, many people not attending church and the collections not covering the cost of repairs. Not happy with this suggestion, Edward instead proposed that the charity land should remain intact and be used for the purposes for which it was donated, and that Mr Hewlett should donate the adjoining land to the parish and pay for the consecration. On a vote, by a slim majority of five votes Mr Hewlett's proposal was accepted. Many of the working-class ratepayers attending the meeting were not happy at the proposed loss of the charity land and, no doubt supported by Edward, it was agreed they would voice their objections to the charity commission in the form of a petition. The charity commission's response is unknown, but the siting of the burial ground today would indicate that Mr Hewlett's proposal went ahead.

From 1888, the local newspapers started reporting on harvest festivals which took place at Haseley. They were very descriptive reports, for example, 'The pulpit was wreathed with oats and yellow daises, some fine bunches of grapes being suspended in the centre' and those who had contributed to the displays were named: 'Thanks to Mrs Oscar Bowen and Mrs Payman for fruit and flowers, and to the villagers who gave flowers and vegetables liberally from their gardens.' At the 1888 service Edward 'forcibly urged upon the congregation the duty of helping as much as possible to reduce the debt on the new burial ground' and on this occasion the offertory amounted to £3-16s-0d [around £300].[138] After the service celebrating the harvest, it became the tradition to send the donated fruit and vegetables to Warneford Hospital in Leamington Spa.

In 1901 the church was closed for three weeks for repairs and to enable a new porch to be built. The porch had been presented to the church by Mr Hewlett of Haseley Manor. A few weeks prior, a rummage sale had been held at Haseley Hall, with the proceeds going towards the repairs and cleaning of the church. Edward and his churchwardens assisted at this event by greeting visitors whilst wives and daughters manned the stalls. A total of £51-9s-0d was raised from the sale and, including donations, the fund raised amounted to £70-17s-7½d [approximately £5,500 today].[139] The updated church opened in time for the annual harvest festival on Sunday 22 September.[140]

That same year Edward discovered a very old recumbent headstone in a very dilapidated condition on the south side of the chancel. He had it restored and found that it was in memory of John Cheney and his wife dated 1738 and contained some interesting monumental designs. There was a Cheney Farm and a Cheney Wood in the parish, which would indicate that John was a member of a local family of some prominence.[141]

Edward's new home was certainly situated in a beautiful part of England and he clearly took his responsibilities towards the church seriously, including taking care of the chancel, extending it and later installing a new window partly dedicated to his mother. He would spend almost half a century in Haseley, but in welcoming their new rector, his new parishioners could not have imagined the number of scandals that would ensue.

Chapter Nine

Convicted of Fraud

HASELEY WAS AROUND EIGHTY MILES FROM Edward's lands and business on the Shropshire/ Wales border, and as a result he was a frequent traveller on the railways. The expanding network was making travelling long distances easier and Edward made full use of it. It is possible that he had never got over being made a laughingstock in court by the Great Western Railway when he made his claim against them and may well have felt that he had been unfairly treated. Maybe he decided to gain recompense or simply saw an opportunity to save money and exploited it, but either way, on Friday 27 September 1867 newspapers across the United Kingdom were reporting on the case of 'A Warwickshire Vicar Convicted of Fraud'.

Edward had attended court in Oswestry the previous day, having been summoned to appear before Mr W. Ormsby Gore MP, Colonel Lovett and Mr B. Owen, the charge being defrauding the Great Western Railway Company by riding from Chester to Hatton Junction, near Haseley, without a ticket. Edward had clearly not learnt from his previous experience of fare dodging. The case drew a great deal of interest and the courtroom was full. As soon as the case was called, Edward's solicitor, Mr Marshall of Birmingham, said that, 'the defendant admitted having ridden but denied the intention to defraud' and he had a proposal which would save the court time. He proposed that if the case was dropped, the defendant was happy to donate any sum they cared to name to any charity in Oswestry they would choose. This strategy had worked when he had been caught two years earlier but not this time; the GWR representative objected to this suggestion, arguing that Edward had been let off a similar charge in March 1865 on payment of £5 to the Salop Infirmary and they were now looking for a conviction.

The facts presented by the GWR were to show that 'the fraud charged against the rev. defendant was one of a series perpetrated in the most ingenious and deliberate manner'. It transpired that Edward had been observed by the railway's employees for some time and it was stated that on 8 August he had purchased a return tourist ticket, number 140, from Leamington to Rhyl which was available to be used on one return journey only during the coming month. Following the purchase of this ticket, and being aware of the previous fraud, instructions were given to the ticket inspectors and guards along the line to observe and take note of the defendant's movements along the route. It was observed that Edward used the ticket on several occasions between the stations the ticket was valid for, including trips to Shrewsbury and Chester, but never quite reaching the final destination and therefore not being asked to give up his ticket as it was assumed that he was subsequently intending to continue to his final destination.

On the return journey he would change at Birmingham and buy a ticket for Hatton Junction, being the nearest station to Haseley. Hatton Junction was the station at which any tickets to Leamington would have to have been surrendered and this way Edward left the station with his tourist ticket still intact.

Despite his actions being identical to those two years earlier, Edward's defence was that he did not understand the rules regarding tourist tickets and did not intentionally commit a fraud. On one occasion he asked an inspector if he could break his journey using a tourist ticket and was told that he could, which he claimed had caused the confusion. He felt that the GWR employees should have pointed out to him that he could not repeatedly use the same ticket and asked for payment as other railway companies do. To quote Edward, 'No, that would not suit this great company – the Great Western Company – the company who can only afford to pay its shareholders one per cent, because it keeps up a lot of fellows to watch parsons' and he declared that if they had alerted him to his mistake he would have willingly made payment.

His comments make you wonder if he was a GWR shareholder. His solicitor suggested that the GWR had 'set man-traps all over the line to catch the defendant' and that they 'wanted to catch a real live clergyman and post him up on placards at the railway stations'. The railway company asked for the highest possible penalty that could be given under law, which would be nothing to someone as rich as Edward, but, with so public a case, show that the company was even prepared to prosecute a clergyman, thereby deterring others from carrying out a similar fraud. The magistrates spoke in strong terms about the enormity of the offence carried out by 'a person occupying the position of the defendant'. He was found guilty of fraud, fined £2 plus costs, the maximum under law, making a total of £5-1s-8d [approximately £300] which was paid immediately.[142]

That was not the end of the matter as, a couple of weeks later, on 9 October a further summons was made where Edward was asked to appear before the Henley-in-Arden magistrates as part of the same fraud for which he had already been prosecuted. This was because part of the chicanery had taken place in another magisterial jurisdiction, and the case was to be heard before the Warwickshire magistrates on 30 October. Prior to the hearing it was agreed that rather than attend court Edward would pay the large sum of £50 [around £3,000 today] to a sick fund established in connection with the GWR. Having already gained a conviction, they saw no benefit in securing a second guilty charge, although ensuring that it was still widely reported in newspapers across the country.

What Bishop Henry Philpott thought of Edward's actions, and now national shame, is not known but there was no change to his duties at Haseley where the church services and other ceremonies continued as if nothing had happened. Although I am sure there were plenty of comments from his parishioners.

Despite the comment being made in court that Edward was a rich man, he was in fact starting to struggle financially due, in part, to some bad business ventures.

Chapter Ten

Mining Interests

Edward had purchased a lead mine in Llangynog formerly owned by Lord Powis. An old Welsh directory states that the mine had been discovered in 1697, contained a vein of lead three yards thick and was worked for forty years by the family, thus making their fortune. It also reports that about 4,000 tons a year of ore had been mined, smelted on the spot and sold at £7 a ton, yielding £20,000 a year. In total the Powis family had probably made a million pounds out of the mine but, by the time of his purchase, there was little lead remaining and Edward soon realised that he was not going to make his fortune from it.

Edward held a short unexpired lease of two or three years on the mine and so, on 15 March 1868, he entered into a contract with a Mr Charles Rule of London who wished to purchase his interests and the plant required to operate it. The price asked for the mine varies in different accounts, Edward claiming later in the bankruptcy court that the sum requested was £1,500 [just under £100,000 today] but that only £500 had ever been paid. As part of the contract, Charles Rule advised Edward that he would receive the outstanding amount if he was able to obtain a renewal of the lease and the mine proved viable. Rule obtained the position of the leaseholder and applied to Lord Powis for a fresh lease of twenty-one years from 9 December 1868. No premium was paid for the lease but there was a rent of £100 a year and a royalty of 1/10th of the ore extracted.[143]

Surprisingly, on this occasion, Edward did not turn to the courts to obtain the money owed. Unbeknown to him, Charles Rule had no intention of operating the mine as a going concern, and in 1879 he and several accomplices were found guilty of using the mine to commit fraud. They had started a newspaper where they praised the mine, stating it was 'one of the most valuable and progressive mines in the principality' and the prospectus stated that royalties paid to Lord Powis had been £800,000, which was a gross exaggeration. Information from Lord Powis's estate account books show that in the sixty-five-year period between 1786 and 1851, the total royalties received for this mine were only £2,850.

Having gained interest, Charles Rule and his accomplices sold shares in the company to an unsuspecting public. One of the witnesses at the fraud trial of Charles Rule and his accomplices, Mr Edwin John, was to testify that he had been employed at Llangynog but left because he found the owners were exaggerating the reports from the mine and altering them. Whilst Edwin John was at the mine, nothing like the claimed 400 tons of lead were raised in one year and the mine only produced about forty tons of lead in the whole of the two and a half years that he was employed there. The mine sometimes seemed to show great promise of yielding but it was never fulfilled, and he never observed anything that led him to believe that the mine would ever be a success. Some of the lead had been mined when he first went to the mine and on Rule's instructions the good lead was put outside the mine and the poorer lead was kept inside covered up. No doubt prompted by Charles Rule, the *Mining Journal* in 1871 was to report that there were hundreds of tons of lead in the mine. At the trial Sir Henry James QC said there had been a gross fraud perpetuated on the public to induce them to take shares and there was ample evidence that the whole purpose of the formation of the company was to sell shares which were of no value. Rule and his fellow defendants were found guilty of committing fraud.[144] There is certainly no evidence to suggest that Edward was in any way involved in the shenanigans but was just a victim himself, as he never received the money owed to him. He was probably just happy to have a loss-making mine taken off his hands.

It was another mine that would cause Edward's downfall, and which once more led him into court on a charge of fraud. He was in partnership with Mr S. Peake in another lead mine in Pontblyddyn, Mold, Flintshire, although this association was to be dissolved in July 1869 due to Peake becoming a bankrupt.[145] Peake had been a fellow exhibitor at the International Exhibition in 1862, at which time he was mining at Berwig Quarry at Minerva near Wrexham. In December 1868 the partners purchased a new property next to their existing mine at Pontblyddyn, possibly using funds from the sale of the Llangynog mine to Charles Rule. To enable them to complete the purchase, in June 1869, they borrowed £900 [approximately £60,000 today] from the Chester Benefit Building Society.

Following the dissolution of the partnership, it became clear that Edward was starting to struggle financially. There was also the added problem of unrest amongst the miners nearby in the area around Mold. A border town in North East Wales, Mold was situated in an area of extensive iron, lead and coal mining, all helping to power the industrial revolution.

Trouble began when two miners were sentenced to imprisonment for attacking the manager of the Leeswood Green Colliery, which was less than a mile from Edward's mine at Pontblyddyn. A popular manager had been replaced by a man called John Young from Durham and his aggressive management style did not sit well with the miners. He also disliked the Welsh and banned the speaking of the Welsh language in the pit. On the day that Young pinned a notice informing the miners that their pay was about to be slashed, the men had simply walked out. They stayed away until the day that the wage cut was due to be implemented, when 200 men returned to the mine to meet with Young, only for their protests to be dismissed. They decided to send him packing literally and marched him to the nearest railway station at Hope, whilst another group of men were at his house packing up his belongings. A couple of police officers came across the men, taking Young to the station and safely escorted him back to Mold. On 6 June seven men were taken to court and the two ringleaders received a prison sentence.

As the two convicted miners were being taken from the court to the railway station for transport to prison, over a thousand miners and their families protested, throwing stones and other missiles at the guards. A troop of soldiers from the King's Own Regiment, based eleven miles from Mold, had been brought in to support the police in anticipation of trouble. Retaliating without warning, the soldiers fired shots into the crowd, killing four people, including two women, and injuring dozens more. The crowd quickly dispersed and by the following morning the blood-soaked streets were empty.

A coroner's inquest was held, and a verdict of justifiable homicide was returned by the Welsh jury. The Riot Act of 1715 had made it a serious crime for members of a crowd of twelve or more to refuse to disperse within an hour of being ordered to do so by a magistrate, although the Act was not read to the rioters at Mold. A further court case ensued relating to the riotous behaviour and five men were sentenced to ten years' penal labour, including a man whose wife had been shot by the soldiers.

Things were clearly unsettled in the area and, although not directly affected, it would have been a worrying time for other local mine owners. Edward and his foreman, a Mr Guest, were struggling to keep their mines viable and immediately fell behind with the mortgage payments, resulting in the building society taking possession of the new mine. The payments were quickly bought up to date and the society relinquished ownership of the mine back to Edward and his foreman. In October 1869 the society was informed that the machinery at the mine, which formed part of the mortgage, had been sold. Mr Tibbetts, a solicitor and the representative of the society, visited the mine and found that the information was correct and that the tramway, machinery sleepers and tips had all gone. They had been sold to a marine store dealer of Buckley named Brannos. Many items had been just given away and in total the property, worth £300 [around £18,000 today], had been sold for just £100.[146]

On 19 November, Mr Tibbetts and a Mr Wood, an accountant for the building society, applied for and were granted a summons against Edward and his foreman on a charge of larceny. Once again Edward was the subject of sensational headlines, with many reporting, 'Serious Charge of Fraud Against a Clergyman.'[147] The case was heard in front of the magistrates, Mr C. B. T. Roper and Mr E. Pemberton at Mold County Hall. Mr Tibbetts appeared for the prosecution and Mr Clarke of Warwick for Edward, who argued that this was not a criminal case and that the magistrates had no jurisdiction in the matter. The prosecution argued that if Mr Muckleston was party to the sale and Mr Guest undertook it, then they should be found guilty of larceny. Mr Peake was absolved of responsibility as he had passed his bankruptcy examination.

After considerable discussion, in which Mr Clarke again submitted that the case could not be taken as one of a criminal nature, Mr Kelly, clerk to the magistrates, said the chief ingredient in a charge of larceny was that of taking goods out of the possession of the owner. As he understood the case, Messrs Peake and Muckleston were in possession of the property. The conditions of the mortgage were that if they got into arrears with their payments, the trustees had the power to receive the rents and profits of the premises, and if they were insufficient then they had the power to sell, and hand over the surplus, if any, to Messrs Peake and Muckleston after having satisfied their claim. At the time the property was removed, Messrs Peake and Muckleston, and not the trustees, were in possession of the premises and, in that case, there was no larceny, in so much as the property was not taken from the possession of the owners. It appeared upon examination of the secretary of the society that Mr Muckleston was not four months in arrears when the proceedings were instituted and upon that point a question was raised upon the complainant's right to take possession, and ultimately the bench ruled that the case was one for a civil action. His solicitor said that Edward had been reduced to his present position, he was almost insolvent, by the dishonesty of his partner and ruinous mining speculations. The bench, acting upon the advice of their clerk, decided they had no jurisdiction in the matter.[148]

Edward may have won on this occasion, but his reprieve was to be short-lived, as financially he was struggling. The lack of four months' payments on the mine had given the upper hand to the Chester Benefit Building Society and they duly advertised the property for sale.[149] John Pickering, on behalf of the mortgagees, was to auction one lot at the Green Dragon Hotel on Monday 21 March at 4pm. This lot comprised three closes of land of just over twelve acres with messuages, erections and buildings thereon situated at Pontblyddyn in the county of Flint late in the holding of Messers Peake and Muckleston and in the occupation of Mr James Hughes, publican, and others. In addition, there was a field or croft of just over two acres situate at Nerquis, in the same county in the occupation of Mrs Oldfield. Also, certain yearly ground rents amounting together to £49-13s-0d, payable or chargeable on portions of the property at Pontblyddyn. The mines and the minerals remained with Edward.[150]

The building society had reclaimed the money that they had loaned on mortgage, but other creditors of Edward's were not as lucky, and his ongoing financial difficulties would have a far-reaching impact, not least on his family.

Chapter Eleven

Bankruptcy

IN 1868, AT THE SAME TIME AS EDWARD WAS
considering investing in his new mine, his sister Mary
Louisa was causing him some difficulty, as she had been
made aware of a clause in their grandfather's will. Her
aunt had passed away on 16 May 1865 and Mary Louisa
engaged a solicitor, Mr Newton of Birmingham, to deal
with the estate and on looking through deeds he found a
bequest which was greatly to Mary Louisa's benefit but to
the disadvantage of her brother.

Her grandfather, Charles Bowdler Muckleston, a
grocer of Shrewsbury, had died on 14 March 1806 and
the clause in his will which interested Mary Louisa stated
that Charles's heir (her father) could use the income
from certain estates to settle a jointure on his wife, not
exceeding £40 a year for life, and allowed for a sum not
exceeding £500 [about £22,000 today] to be shared and
settled amongst any younger children of his marriage. As
had happened in many previous Muckleston generations,
the eldest surviving son inherited the lands and property
but this clause in Charles's will provided for the younger

siblings, Elizabeth and Mary Louisa, giving them a start in life. The payment was to be made on their marriage or upon attaining the age of twenty-one.[151]

Mary was now thirty-nine years old and although she had never married was well past the age when she should have received her inheritance. Her sister Elizabeth had received monies from the estate as part of her marriage settlement and as such it could be assumed that, having benefitted from the estate, she did not have a claim. It is possible that Elizabeth did not know about the clause either or surely she would have mentioned it to her sister. Mary Louisa was totally dependent on her family for financial support as she had no income and controlling money of her own would make a great difference to the way she would be able to live her life. It is possible that Edward was unaware of the bequest in his grandfather's will, but he was certainly in no hurry to fulfil his obligation to his sister. Mary Louisa spent three years asking her brother for her inheritance, as he owned the estates from which this payment had been bequeathed, each time without a successful outcome. Mary Louisa felt she had no option but to take him to court.

As the case involved property, Mary Louisa lodged her claim in the Court of Chancery, presided over by the Lord Chancellor and his deputies, which dealt with disputes relating to equity, trusts, land law and estates. In February 1868, Mary Louisa, who was now living at Benbow Place in Shrewsbury with her widowed mother, brought her complaint before Lord Chancellor, Frederick Baron Chelmsford, requesting that the trust in her grandfather's will be satisfied through either mortgage or sale of the lands at Coton Hill which had originally been designated to provide the bequest.[152] Her submission to the court took the form of several statements efficiently explaining her claim, each one numbered and detailing everything which, she believed, led to her having a genuine claim against the estate. She stated that her brother had inherited these lands in 1845 during their father's lifetime and that the indenture at that time included a charge against the estate of the payment of £160 a year [about £10,500 today] payable to their mother. When her brother received his inheritance, she was twenty years old and nothing had been mentioned about the clause in her grandfather's will from which she should profit. In conjunction with her solicitor she put forward a very structured argument including details of every document and life event which impacted on the situation.

Mary Louisa was entitled to half of the designated £500 through her grandfather's will; she and her solicitor calculated that, if the money had been invested as requested, at the age of twenty-one she should have received the sum of £414-3s-4d including interest. Had she received this money when she became entitled and invested it, then it would now be worth £630-8s-0d [around £37,000 today] and this was the amount of her claim, plus the cost of bringing the case to court.

Edward and his co-defendants, his cousin Reverend John Muckleston and Thomas Porter Lyon, both of whom also had an interest in the Coton Hill estate, were duly served papers. They were given eight days to respond to a list of questions based on Mary Louisa's statements, risking the threat of imprisonment should they fail to do so. They could hardly argue with the facts put before them, but they did query that whether, along with all the other claims on the estate, that there was enough equity to cover the claim in full. Ultimately, Edward was the only person deemed to be liable under Mary Louisa's petition.

Things were slow to progress through Chancery, but almost a year and a half after making the claim, Mary Louisa won her case and an order was granted on 8 July 1869 confirming that the court had awarded Mary Louisa Muckleston the sum of £343-14s-9d [about £21,500 today] plus five per cent interest per annum to be added effective from 21 June 1851, the date of her father's death. Edward failed to fulfil the courts demand to pay the money to his sister and on 4 December 1869 the Court of Chancery sent a writ to the Sheriff of Warwickshire requiring him to deal with the matter. The sheriff was expected to locate Edward, obtain the money by any means necessary and submit it to the court. On the back of the writ, Edward Wood, the sheriff, had identified Edward as the Rector of Haseley, but had also written, 'the within named Edward Muckleston hath not any goods or chattels or any lay fee in any Bailiwick wherof I can cause to be made the sum of money and interest'.

This was not the first time that Edward Wood had been sent to the rectory at Haseley. Another case had also been going through Chancery around the same time as Mary Louisa's. This was Clarke v Muckleston where Richard Clarke also won his case and the sheriff had been sent to obtain £2,034-7s-10d [around £130,000 today] from Edward less than two months earlier. He had also left empty-handed on that occasion, reporting that Edward did not have the means to pay anything.

Just one day before the writ relating to his sister was issued, Edward had filed for bankruptcy; the initial hearing being arranged to take place on 17 December at twelve noon.[153] The claim from his sister, the debts from his mining interests, mainly owed to companies based in Sheffield, and those to many others were placed before the Bankruptcy Court in Birmingham.

> The humble petition of Edward Muckleston of Haseley in the County of Warwick, clerk in Holy Orders and until recently in partnership at Pontblyddyn near Mold in the County of Flint as a colliery proprietor.
>
> That your petitioner having resided for six calendar months next immediately preceding the date of this petition within the district of the honorable court that is to say at Haseley aforesaid is unable to meet his engagements with his creditors. Your petitioner therefore humbly prays that adjudication of bankruptcy may be made against him. Signed by the petitioner on the third day of December 1869 in the presence of William Henry Harris, Solicitor Birmingham agent to the solicitor in the matter of this petition.
>
> I the undersigned a registrar of the Court of Bankruptcy for the Birmingham district upon good proof before me this day taken do find that the said Edward Muckleston has become bankrupt within the true intent and meaning of the laws of bankruptcy and I do therefore declare and adjudge him bankrupt accordingly. O D Tudor registrar.[154]

Although he would certainly have preferred not to be in this position, Edward's timing could not have been better as he would now almost certainly avoid imprisonment. The Bankruptcy and Debtors Acts of 1869 saw significant changes in the law resulting in an increase in the number of bankruptcies being declared. Debtors' prisons were full of rats, lice and fleas, and the prisoners were denied the basic necessities of life, such as food, water and clothing, unless they were provided by their friends, and around twenty-five per cent of inmates died as a result of these conditions. Other countries had legislation limiting incarceration for debt to one year, but England had no such law and when the Fleet prison closed in 1842 it was found that some prisoners had been there for more than thirty years, as debtors could be imprisoned until their debts were paid, or the creditors agreed to their release. The 1869 Acts brought an end to these prisons, as the new Act abolished imprisonment for debt (with a few exceptions) but included punishment for fraudulent debtors, such as someone failing to pay a creditor if they were able to do so. The Acts came into force on 1 January 1870.[155]

The first step in the bankruptcy process was to appoint an assignee of the estate. This was someone who would gather together all of the remaining assets that the bankrupt still owned, and Walter Newton Fisher, Accountants of Birmingham, were appointed to this role. Edward's many creditors were represented by Mr C. B. Hodgson of Hodgson and Son.

There were several meetings regarding the bankruptcy; Edward was not required to attend them all, and opted not to, but was represented by his solicitor Mr Harris of the firm of Reece and Harris. During one such meeting, Mr Marshall, acting on behalf of a Mr Greenhough, who was claiming £1,030 [approximately £65,000 today] from

Edward, explained that his client had lost one of the two promissory notes for £500.[156] The list of debtors supplied by Edward was consulted and it was noted that he had listed the debt as £1,000 plus £30 interest, and it was agreed to keep the debt on the list in anticipation of either the note being found or Edward agreeing that it was indeed a true debt. Ensuring that every detail was investigated, Mr Hodgson asked for the deficiency and trading accounts for the mine for the last three years and Mr Wing, who was an accountant and secretary for the Sheffield Waggon Company, one of Edward's major creditors, and keen to get the situation resolved as soon as possible, kept pressing the court for a quick resolution.[157]

Mr Hodgson calculated the debts to be nearly £12,000 [approximately £750,000 today] with a deficit of nearly £10,000.[158] The majority of the estates Edward owned had been mortgaged and one of the largest debts was for a sum of £2,400 [approximately £150,000 today] owed to Messers Thomas Bloxham and John Fortescue, who had loaned Edward this amount of money as a mortgage against his estates at Worthen.[159] The provision that his mother Elizabeth, then aged eighty-one, was to continue receiving her annual allowance was protected despite her son's bankruptcy.[160] There were frequent adjournments to allow Mr Harris to consult Edward as he could not always immediately answer questions that were put to him. Eventually it was deemed prudent to call Edward to court to enable a private examination to take place.

Edward attended the court in April[161] and was examined for over an hour by Mr Hodgson. During the questioning Edward explained that he was formerly possessed of a lead mine on Lord Powis's estate at Craiga

Mowen in Wales which, five years before, he had sold to a Mr Rule for £1,500, but Mr Rule had only paid £500 of this sum, refusing to pay any more because, he said, it was not a legal transfer. Mr Rule was last heard of residing at Cannon Street, London. When Edward was challenged by Mr Hodgson as to why he had not previously mentioned this debt due to him, he said, 'I thought it no use as Rule

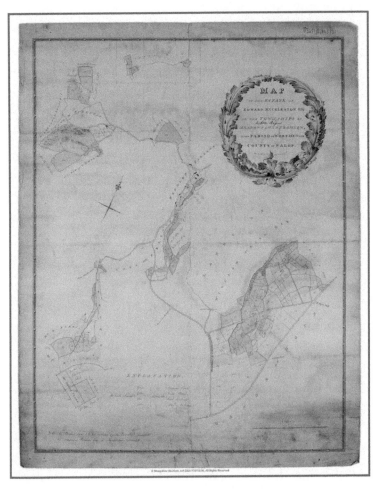

Estate map of Edward Muckleston's lands.

said he would never pay.' More questions were asked but Edward did not have all the answers to hand and Mr Hodgson, feeling that he did not have the full picture of his financial situation, asked the judge to order Edward to furnish, within a week, a list of his tenants, the acreage and all particulars regarding leases, etc.[162] Mr Hodgson wanted to move forward with liquidating his assets and required this information to enable the sales documents to be put together. This included the drawing-up of an estate map depicting some of Edward's land holdings.

Preliminary announcements of 'a sale of valuable manorial lands' appeared in several newspapers during the months of May, June and July, with the sale planned to take place on 11 August 1870 at the George Hotel, Shrewsbury, as most of the properties were situated in the county.

Edward's bankruptcy now impacted on his wider family, not just his sister Mary Louisa, who had the writ granted by Chancery outstanding, but also his other sister Elizabeth, who, along with her husband William Lyon and their three children, were living at the very low annual rent of just £60 [less than £4,000 today] in Ford Hall, a property which was now to be sold. The family had a lease which did not expire until Lady Day 1874[163] and so they had some security until then. Their mother's income also came from the estates and when the sale particulars were produced, it was made clear to any potential buyers that the continuation of the payment of £40 a year was to be made to Elizabeth Muckleston for the remainder of her life.[164]

The 'Conditions of Sale' produced regarding the sale to be held at the George Hotel Shrewsbury on Thursday 11 August 1870 were as follows:

Lots:

1. Freehold Messuage situated in Quarry Place, Shrewsbury, now in the occupation of Mrs Stansfield at a yearly rent of £66 or thereabouts.

2. Superior country mansion at Ford with about two acres of land. Ornamental pleasure grounds including a fishpond, orchard and garden, stabling and commodious outbuildings now in the occupation of William Lyon Esq, who holds a lease which expires on Lady Day 1874 at a very low rent of £60 per annum. The lot is copyhold and is held of the Lord of the Manor of Ford.

3. Thirty-one properties in the parish of Bromlow, Worthen, Pentervin and Shropshire in general, from houses, cottage, farms and land total acreage 215 and annual rental of £322-7s-0d.

4. Lordship of Aston Rogers all commons, waste grounds, mines, minerals, manorial and other rights, lands and hereditaments belonging to the manor in the towns, parishes, fields and hamlets of Aston Rogers, Bromlow, Meadow Town, Medlicott and elsewhere in the county of Salop.

5. Wood Farm near Meadow Town in Bromlow substantial farm buildings and forty-one acres of land including over twelve acres known as Muckleston's Wood – occupied by Mr Jno Woodhouse at annual rent of £50.

6. Two houses and gardens at Aston Hill, total yearly rent of £9.

7. Lyde House and Mynd Cop near to Meadow Town – farm cottage and homestead with

various closes and parcels of land total acreage of over thirty-three acres occupied by Thomas Hayward at the yearly rent of £52-10s-0d.

8. Penybryn Farm situated in Penybryn in the parish of Llanfechan in the county of Montgomery over 131 acres in the occupation of David Thomas at the yearly rent of £134.

Lot 3 to be offered first and if lot 4 is not sold separately it would be offered with lot 5.

Charles Muckleston's will dated 14 April 1799 mentions lots 3, 4, 5 and 6. And it is a condition of sale of these lots that Elizabeth Muckleston should receive an annuity of £40 per annum for life from these lots.'

Lot 2, the house at Ford, was sold to Henry Lee, a farmer of Ensdon near Montford Bridge, for £1,200 [approximately £75,000 today] and he allowed the family to continue to rent the house.[165] Although her husband died in 1880, Elizabeth remained at Ford Hall until her death in 1897. The estates and Lordship, which had passed down several generations of the Muckleston family, were now in the hands of others. Edward just needed everything to be confirmed by the court and he was undoubtably relieved when, on Tuesday 27 September, Birmingham District Bankruptcy Court gave notice that they had granted the discharge of his bankruptcy. It had taken ten long months to sort out the financial mess which Edward had got himself into and his family had suffered along with him. There was, however, a provision from the court that there was the right to appeal against the discharge and it would turn out that Edward had not been completely honest regarding his assets.[166]

Edward had an extensive cellar containing port, sherry and claret, and had failed to mention it or list it as an asset. Someone, who must have been quite close to him, brought it to the court's attention and more than six months after his discharge, a special meeting of the creditors was called.[167] The 110th section of the Act stated that even when the bankrupt applied for a full discharge, if any of the creditors felt that the bankrupt had not made a full disclosure of his assets, that they could ask for the bankrupt to be re-examined. Was it his sister Mary Louisa or his servant, both creditors, who had reported his undeclared assets, or had he made the mistake of offering someone else a glass of fine old port and had that person wondered how a bankrupt could afford such luxury? Regardless of how they found out, this was an asset which could be sold to the benefit of the creditors and it was duly advertised for sale.

The above advertisement was to appear in several newspapers.

Although the outcome was not as bad as Mr Hodgson had thought when he reported a shortfall of £10,000, those with mortgages had their debts paid on sale of the relevant properties they were secured on, but those creditors with unsecured debts, such as his sister Mary Louisa, only received 8s-8d in the pound, just over forty per cent of what they were owed. There was also an issue to be resolved regarding one of the debts secured by a mortgage.

The matter which Mary Louisa's solicitor, Mr Newton, had been looking into on her behalf in 1865 was also caught up in Edward's bankruptcy process. Mary Louisa and Edward had an aunt named Mary Shaw née Muckleston, their father's sister, who died on 16 May 1865. Mary was a widow who was also childless and who, probably concerned as to how her unmarried niece would cope on the death of her mother, left her entire estate to Mary Louisa. When her nephew Edward needed money, he had asked his aunt for help and she loaned him two sums, one of £400 [about £25,000 today] and another for £1,100 [about £65,000 today]. To secure the debt, he handed her several deeds and confirmed everything in the following letter written on 25 October 1864:

When I last had the conversation with you about the interest, it was agreed between us that if I gave you 5 per cent for the use of your £1,100 you would be satisfied. I gave you the title deeds of Pen y Bank farm on your £400 as double security. I trust therefore, as I pay you so regularly, you will not put me to the great expense of mortgaging the Bromlow property... ... ...Besides the deeds now in your possession are of more value than all the money I have now from you.

Edward had clearly been struggling financially for several years before his final financial collapse and on her aunt's death Mary Louisa inherited the £1,500 debt [approximately £95,000 today] plus interest owed by her brother. During the bankruptcy proceedings it came to light that four years after taking the loan from his aunt, Edward used the same property as security with Messers Dixon, Bankers of Chester, without telling them of Mary Shaw's charge on the property. He owed them £4,591 [approximately £285,000 today] and gave the deeds over on 24 April 1868. It appears that due to several changes there were various sets of deeds, created at the time of marriages and inheritance, and this is how Edward was able to give a set to his aunt and another to the bankers. During the bankruptcy process the bankers filed a motion requesting to have priority against the property over Mary Louisa. Being unable to resolve the situation with the bankers, having succeeded once before and feeling she had a very good case, following the finalisation of her brother's bankruptcy Mary Louisa took the case to Chancery in August 1870.[168] As before, it took eighteen months for the case to be completed through this court and after several hearings, she won her case.[169] The decision was made that the letter sent by Edward and retained by Mary Shaw along with the deeds was in fact an equitable mortgage. The outcome was that Mary Louisa had first claim on what was left of the Coton Hill and Pen y Bank estates and the bankers a second claim.[170]

Having lost the case, the bankers appealed on the grounds that the letter which Edward had written to his aunt did not mention the Coton Hill estate.[171] The judge who heard the appeal said that Mrs Shaw would have been unlearnt in the law and would have had no reason to question the validity of the deeds. He confirmed the earlier decision that the Pen y Bank estate should be used as security and go to Mary Louisa but agreed that the bankers did have a priority claim on the Coton Hill estate. Mary Louisa was now in a position of being able to sell the Pen y Bank estate but had to wait to see how much was left from the sale of the more valuable Coton Hill estate once the bankers had taken what they were owed.

Edward had a weight taken from his shoulders, but his family had suffered in the process; fortunately, Mary Louisa, now forty-eight years old, was tenacious and managed to salvage something for herself to secure her own financial future, and in 1874 the Pen y Bank estate was sold nearly nine years after she inherited it from her aunt. Their mother had died on 28 June 1873 and the estates were now free of the liability of making payments to her.

TO BE SOLD, pursuant to a Decree of the High Court of Chancery, made in a Cause of DIXON v. MUCKLESTON, with the approbation of his Honour, the Master of the Rolls,

BY MR. WILLIAM HALL,

the person appointed by the said Judge, at the Gogerddan Arms and Lion Royal Hotel, Aberystwith, in the County of Cardigan, on Wednesday, the 6th day of May 1874, at Four o'clock in the afternoon, in one Lot,

A FREEHOLD ESTATE, called Pen-y-bank, situate in the parish of Llanfihangel Gener Glyn, near Aberystwith, in the County of Cardigan, comprising about 61A. 1R. 33P. of PASTURE, ARABLE, and WOOL LAND, with a FARMHOUSE and BUILDINGS, now in the occupation of Mr. William Richard.

Particulars and conditions of Sale and further information may be obtained of Mr. J. S. NEWTON, Solicitor, of Temple Chambers, 50, New Street, Birmingham; of Messrs. BELFROGE and MIDDLETON, Solicitors, 36, Bedford Row, London, W.C.; of Messrs. W. and H. T. BROWN and ROGERS, Solicitors, of Chester; of Messrs. MILNE, RIDDLE, and MELLOR, Solicitors, 2, Harcourt Buildings, Temple, London; of the AUCTIONEER, at his Offices, Shrewsbury, and at the place of Sale.

Dated this 14th day of March, 1874.

Sale notice relating to the Pen-y-Bank estate.

This was not the end of the matter for Edward, as a clause in the 1861 Bankruptcy Act stated that, 'should the bankrupt be a benefice clergyman the assignees may apply for and obtain a sequestration of the profits of the benefice of such bankrupt... ... ...provided always that the sequestrator shall allow out of the benefice to the bankrupt whilst he performs the duties of the parish such an annual sum payable quarterly, as the Bishop of the Diocese shall direct... ... ...to appoint to such bankrupt the like stipend as by law he might have appointed to a curate duly licenced to such benefice'. Bishop Philpott was required by law to appoint someone to manage the affairs of the benefice of Haseley and out of the profits to just allow Edward to receive the sum of money he would pay a curate, with the rest of the profits going towards paying off the debts not paid in full as a result of his bankruptcy. The bishop appointed a Mr Alfred C. Hooper, a gentleman of Worcester, to be sequestrator, asking him to pay Edward an allowance of £80 a year [about £5,000 today] and he also allowed Edward to remain in the rectory.[172]

Mr Hooper was responsible for collecting the tithes from the parishioners, any other income from the parish and the rent from the two farmers, who were at that time renting farmland belonging to the glebe. These farmers were a Mr Dodwell, who paid a rent of £42 per annum [around £2,600 today], and a Mr Bray, whose annual rent was £33 [about £2,000 today]. Hooper was able to claim his expenses and then handed over any additional profits to Edward's creditors and those who had writs issued by Chancery. Rather embarrassingly, a notice was pinned to the church door in January 1870, advising the parishioners that Mr Hooper had these duties. It would take almost eight years for the debts to be cleared and Mr Hooper to obtain written confirmation from Richard Clarke, Mary Louisa Muckleston and Mr W. A. Fisher, who had acted for the creditors during the bankruptcy hearing, that the debts had been settled.[173]

I suspect that Mr Hooper was pleased to be able to pin yet another notice to the church door saying that the management of the benefice was once more in the hands of the rector. In 1878 Edward wrote to Mr Hooper complaining that some of the work Hooper had arranged to be carried out on the farm buildings and gate, was of a very poor quality and that he, Edward, knew someone who could do a far better job. I suspect that this was not the only letter Mr Hooper had received from Edward as I can imagine that he had had to suffer Edward complaining and interfering constantly during the years he had been managing the benefice. You can almost sense his relief when the very next day he was able to respond:

17 October 1878

Dear Sir,

I have completely done with the Rectory of Haseley as sequester and you must excuse my saying that you must manage its affairs yourself.

I am yours faithfully,

A. C. Hooper

Having been made bankrupt and living on the equivalent of a curate's salary, you would think there would be little to attract a member of the opposite sex but, as always, Edward was about to surprise us.

Chapter Twelve

Family Man

EDWARD WAS NOW A BANKRUPT, AND ONE WHO HAD been found guilty of fraud at that, not an attractive marriage proposition you would think. However, at the age of fifty-two, he managed to find himself a wife who was half his age. The wedding took place on 27 July 1871 at St George's Church, Hanover Square, London. His bride was Emily Holmes, the twenty-six-year-old daughter of Trafford Holmes MD and his wife Ann Taylor Booth (both deceased). The marriage was by banns and Edward gave his address as Hanover Square, with his bride giving her address as Christ Church, Forest Hill, London. The ceremony was carried out by Charles Kirby Robinson, Master of St Catherine's College, Cambridge and their witnesses were the bride's sister, Julia Morgan Payler, and her two uncles, Nathaniel Holmes and the Reverend Henry Cautley Holmes. Edward erroneously entered his father's occupation as Captain in the army instead of Lieutenant, which was the highest rank he had obtained, but then his father had encouraged everyone to call him Captain Muckleston and Edward was just perpetuating this deception.

Emily was born on 29 April 1845 in Southedge House, Hipperholme, near Halifax, Yorkshire, and was the eldest child of Trafford Holmes and his wife, having one younger sister named Julia.[174] Just four months after her sister's birth, their mother died at Torquay in Devon, where she had gone for her health; she was just twenty-two years old. Their father, a doctor who mainly worked as a general practitioner, never remarried. At the age of fourteen,[175] Emily also lost her father, he was just forty-six years old, and after his death Emily and Julia were sent to a small private school in Thurlow Place, Lambeth, Surrey, where they were two of just five pupils. At the time of the 1871 census they were both staying in a lodging house at 25 Montague Street, Bloomsbury, London and were of independent means. Three months before Emily married Edward, her younger sister Julia had married the cumbersomely named Reverend Frederick Payler Morgan Payler.

In his will Trafford Holmes had set up a trust fund for his two daughters.[176] He had requested that all his real estate be sold and the money arising from this sale to be invested in Parliamentary Stocks, Public Funds of Great Britain, or any other government or real securities within England as his executors saw fit. His nominated executors were his brother Nathaniel Holmes, a gentleman, and his brother-in-law Samuel Bottomley, a worsted spinner and manufacturer. They were required to use the interest from the trusts along with the rents and interests from properties and investments to which his two daughters had become entitled on the death of their mother 'to pay for their comfortable and respectful maintenance and education'. Once Julia reached the age of twenty-one, the capital of the trust was divided into two equal parts and given to the sisters.[177] In December 1868 Emily and Julia came into their inheritance.

One of Julia and Emily's uncles was a vicar who may well have thought that it was about time his nieces married and looked around for potential candidates amongst the clergy. You can see the attraction for Edward, the opportunity of a bride who at least had a comfortable inheritance and Emily may have been worried about still being single at the age of twenty-six. Even if Emily was unaware of Edward's difficulties, her uncle would surely have known about the various scandals, including his bankruptcy, as they had been widely publicised.

The couple made their home in the rectory at Haseley and their first child, a daughter who they named Mabel Emily, was born there on 12 June 1872, ten and a half months after their wedding. Edward baptised his daughter on 11 August in the church at Haseley.

When Mabel was three years old, the family was complete with the birth of a son, Charles Edward Muckleston, on the 7 October 1875. He was to be known as Charley to his family.[178] Just over six weeks after his birth,[179] Charles's baptism was also carried out at Haseley, but this time with a little more ceremony as the child's uncle, Edward's brother-in-law, the Reverend Frederick Payler Morgan Payler, curate of Marton in Warwickshire, was called on to officiate.

Although Edward's mother, Elizabeth, had almost certainly met her granddaughter, she passed away on the 28 June 1873 at the age of eighty-seven, and never got to meet the grandson who would continue the Muckleston surname for this branch of the family. Elizabeth's marriage settlement and various jointures had provided her a regular income, but these died with her and there was little for Elizabeth to leave, resulting in her personal estate being valued at less than £100 [around £6,000 today]. This small sum was left to her unmarried daughter, Mary Louisa.

Emily kept close links with her family and in 1875,[180] Edward assisted her uncle, Reverend Henry Cautley Holmes, at the marriage of her cousin Jane Bottomley to Rufus Michell Esq at St Michael's Church at Shelf near Halifax.

Emily was musical and played the organ in the church at Haseley and led the choir. Both of her children also had similar talents, especially Mabel, and the local newspapers frequently mentioned concerts where Emily and Mabel participated in the entertainment. Mabel attended Hill House School in Warwick, an establishment to educate 'Ladies', with the principals being Mrs and Misses Fosbroke. In the advertisements for the school they would say, 'most highly recommended by Indian Officers, Clergymen and Gentlemen for its excellent educational system, healthiness of situation, and the constant care bestowed by Mrs Fosbroke on the health and comfort of her pupils'. In July 1884 Mabel, aged twelve, won the 'Little Girls Prize' and the mayor, Major Fosbery, attended the prize-giving. In his speech he demonstrated the attitude towards education for women in that era by saying, 'The education of a woman in cookery, needlework, and all that which tended to make her a good manageress of a household, was a great benefit', and he advised any young girl, if she 'desired to fulfil woman's mission, to become the manageress of a household and a family, to cultivate the hand as much as the head, then the one aided by the other, would make them ready for their future, and make them indeed fitting helpmeets for man'. The local doctor, Mr Tibbitts, thanked the mayor and said that he heartily agreed with his Worship in his views on education, with cookery being far more important than science or art.[181] While at school Mabel passed several music examinations including the Trinity College, London, Examination in Music (Practical) at the age of fourteen[182] by scoring 62 out of 90.[183] She passed the same exam at senior level four years later.[184] She also enjoyed cycling.

Her brother Charles's education took place at St John's School in Leatherhead, Surrey. This school had been founded in 1851 for the sons of poor clergy and its founder was the clergyman Ashby Haselwood. Originating in London, it moved to Leatherhead in 1872. It remained a charity school under the headmastership of Arthur Rutty (1883–1909), when the school gained all the characteristics of a private school and started to attract fee-paying pupils while remaining loyal to the sons of poor clergy. Charles was educated under Mr Rutty attending the school from around 1887 to 1894, where he demonstrated his sporting prowess by playing both cricket and football for the school. In 1890 he gained a first-class honour in the University of Cambridge Local Examinations[185] and appeared in a list of successful students under the age of sixteen. Charles was destined for Cambridge University; the master of St Catherine's College had officiated at Edward and Emily's wedding, and this was the college which Charles attended. Following in his father's footsteps, he obtained his BA in Theology in June 1900[186] and six months later was ordained a deacon by the Lord Bishop of Chester at the parish church of St John the Baptist in Chester[187] and was then licensed to the curacy of Sandbach in Cheshire.[188]

Educating his children would have been costly and maybe that is why Edward turned to providing testimonials such as this one for Tooth Block, which appeared in a variety of newspapers for several years from November 1883 until 1890:[189]

> **O. S.** OSCAR SUTTON AND Co., PRESTON.
> **TOOTH BLOCK,** 1s. and **2s. 6d.**
> "The best and safest Dentifrice."
> Hundreds of Testimonials.
> The Rev. E. Muckleston, M.A., Haseley Rectory, Warwick, writes:—"I have had great experience in all kinds of materials for cleaning my teeth; I must say, with truth, that I prefer yours to all others."
> Sold by all Chemists and Perfumers. Where there is any difficulty in obtaining them, they will be sent post free on receipt of 1s. or 2s. 6d. in stamps.

And this one for butter powder which first appeared in March 1884:[190]

> **TOMLINSON & HAYWARD, LINCOLN.**
> TESTIMONIAL—
> Haseley Rectory and Haseley Glebe Farm, Warwick, January 31st, 1884.
> Sirs,—During the winter I could not obtain from my Cows a good sample of Butter, owing to bad tastes which I could not prevent. By chance I read an advertisement of your Butter Powder, and having heard a good deal about it, procured some, and the first trial exceeded my expectations by making the butter just as I wished it to be, proving the Powder to be a most useful article for Dairy Keepers, in removing the bad tastes of Turnips, Cakes, Sour Grass, &c., from their Butter.—Yours truly,
> EDWARD MUCKLESTON, M.A.
> P.S.—We find that your Powder purifies the second skimming, which, before we tried it, was generally of very little value.

His bankruptcy well behind him, Edward made another attempt to become involved in business, obtaining a position as one of five directors of George Gunn (Limited) Cereal Food Manufacturers. He was listed as such when the company advertised 6,000 shares at £5 each to be sold to raise £30,000 [around two and a half million pounds today] in July 1890. The owner, Leonard Gunn, had agreed to stay as managing director for at least five years and the services of the manager, Mr Albert Greenberg, had been secured. The company produced a wide range of cereals and had been supplying the Queen's household with breakfast cereals for over twenty-five years.[191] The sale of shares was to prove unsuccessful and Mr Leonard Gunn was declared bankrupt the following year, the business was closed and the assets sold.[192] Leonard was probably a relation of Major George Gunn Munro, whose daughter's wedding Edward had conducted in 1849. As it was a limited company, the impact on Edward was likely to have been restricted to the loss of his shareholding.

Edward was married to a respectable woman and had two children to be proud of, but his relationships with others would always have their challenges, and both before and after his marriage, things would not run smoothly for Edward in Haseley.

Chapter Thirteen

Servants and Employees

Edward had clearly learnt nothing from his poor relationships at Ford and instead of seeing Haseley as a fresh start, he simply carried on in his usual selfish manner.

When he moved to his new parish in 1865 Edward was a single man; the fourteen-roomed rectory at Haseley required cleaning and he also needed someone to cook and care for him. There was nothing to see but fields and the nearest town was over an hour's walk away, although there was a railway station at Hatton a mile distant, and having just Edward in the house to speak to, it needed someone special to take on the role of servant in this rural location. Edward found this person in Mary Ann Blower, a single woman who, according to the 1871 census, had been born around 1828 at Westbury in Shropshire.[193]

In 1851, twenty-six-year-old Mary Blower was working as a servant for John Muckleston, a grocer and tea dealer of Wyle Cop, Shrewsbury. John was a distant relative of Edward's, in fact he was a third cousin twice removed, but they would have known each other as family due to the uniqueness of their surname. John had been declared bankrupt in 1850 and in 1855 was imprisoned due to a debt of £106 owed to George and Richard Russell. Thankfully he was released after three weeks by order of the sheriff, having gone through the Exchequer Court where his debt was discharged. Two years later he spent a further six weeks in custody again on a charge of debt made once again by Richard Russell, this time claiming to be owed £26. The second charge was also dismissed but, due to his financial situation, John may have struggled to continue to employ a servant and recommended her to his relative Edward.

The keeping of domestic servants was 'the dividing line between the working classes and those of a higher social scale'.[194] Many would agree with this comment, including Josiah Crawley, the perpetual curate in Anthony Trollope's *Last Chronicle of Barset*, published in 1867, who struggled to keep a maid on an income of £130 per annum despite the carpets being rags and the furniture shabby and broken. The life of a general servant was often a solitary one but life in a vicarage would be better than working for a shopkeeper, who often expected assistance in the shop or a farmer who needed help in feeding animals. Many of the more professional classes, such as doctors, bank managers and clergymen, would aim to employ three servants, as this was considered the minimum necessary if the household was to be 'complete in all its functions'. These would normally consist of a cook, housemaid and parlour maid. Servants were a drain on income and the poorer clergy often settled for a single general servant.

Mary was engaged on a salary of £16 a year [approximately £1,000 today], together with her board, which was slightly below the typical wage of £20–£25 a year for a housekeeper.[195] For this sum of money, Mary was expected to light the fires, prepare the breakfast, clean Edward's boots, make the beds and clean the slops, sweep and dust the rooms, prepare his lunch, black lead the hearth, clean the windows, prepare dinner and wash up, and maybe even run the occasional errand. Mary did have some money of her own and was either a very generous person or fell for Edward's charm, as she loaned him the sum of £200 [about £12,500 today] at some point between her engagement as his servant and his bankruptcy in 1869, when she appeared as one of his creditors. Along with his other creditors, she only received eight shillings in the pound, resulting in the substantial loss of £120, the equivalent of seven and a half years' wages. You can only wonder what made Mary remain at Haseley; maybe she had nowhere to go or thought that by remaining he would one day be able to pay her back for her loyalty and generosity. Whatever the situation, Mary would remain with Edward until her death.

Ten years after moving to Haseley, Edward was summoned to attend the county court situated in Northgate Street in the centre of Warwick,[196] in a case to be heard by Mr R. Harrington. Justice had been served in this building since 1758 and the summons was heard in one of the two octagonal courtrooms.[197] This hearing would show that, despite a decade in the parish, all was not well between Edward and his parishioners and provided much entertainment to those in the public gallery, causing much laughter in court. The headline in the local newspaper read 'A Clergyman and his Surplice'. The summons was brought by Mrs Gubbins, the forty-four-year old wife of Joseph Gubbins, a grocer and farmer, who in court was to claim she lived on 'her own estate' at Haseley. Mrs Gubbins was claiming three shillings for washing Edward's surplice on two separate occasions, in December 1873 and March 1874, and had still not been paid for her work. The surplice is a white linen or cotton tunic Edward would have worn over his cassock and, as such, would have required extra care and attention when washing to ensure the garment reflected the importance of this part of the clergyman's vestment. Mrs Gubbins felt a precedent had been set, as Reverend Griffiths, in an adjoining parish, had always paid her directly for the same service.

Instead of taking steps to try and avoid such a public airing of the differences between himself and his parishioner, Edward was happy to defend the case, which he saw as a matter of principle.

Taking her place in the witness box, Mrs Gubbins testified how she sought assurances from Edward that he would pay her for her work, as she had been told by others that he had previously failed to do so, but on sending him a bill she was insulted when it was returned with a note on the bottom and felt her only recourse was to bring a summons against him. The note was viewed in court and indicated that Edward had denied liability and had suggested that an interview would remove misapprehension, and he reminded Mrs Gubbins of a favour he had done her which he feared forgotten. The judge, sitting in his chair overlooking the court, saw nothing wrong with the note and felt that she was being overly sensitive.

Grasping the rail of the dock directly facing the judge, this man of principle, certain that he had right on his side, explained that there was a parish charity of £7-10s-0d [around £500 today] to pay for surplice washing and other expenses. He had told Mrs Gubbins that the churchwarden would pay when she first took the washing and he had refused to pay on principle. Edward said that he could produce the church payment books to show that washing the surplices had been paid by the parish for twenty-five years and he had advised a Mr Morris, who came to see him on Mrs Gubbins' behalf, that this was the case. Mr Sanderson, acting for Edward, explained that things were not as rosy as they should be in the parish, as there was much ill feeling from the parishioners towards the rector. The churchwarden, who had recently died, had been opposed to Edward, going as far as to refuse to attend church even though it was his duty to do so, and it was their opinion that Mrs Gubbins had been encouraged by this churchwarden to bring the case against Edward to cause him annoyance.

In his summing up, Judge Harrington said that he could not believe that Edward, a man of the cloth, would perjure himself over a matter of this kind, but at the same time he regretted that the amount had not been paid for the sake of the peace of the parish. Sharing his thoughts on the matter, the judge had some harsh words for Edward and said that he thought the course that Edward had adopted was much to be regretted, considering the position he occupied in the parish: 'A clergyman of the Church of England might well consent to the imposition of a charge of 6s a year [approximately £20 today] rather than do anything to promote ill-feeling in the parish.' He went on to say that, 'Whether liable to pay or not, if he ordered the work to be done as his own, he would be liable to pay for it, and it would be for him to settle the matter with those who were really liable. However unjust the charge may be, he thought the clergyman of the parish may have permitted himself to be imposed upon for such a trifling amount rather than to do anything which was likely to augment the ill will and bad feeling which unfortunately existed in the parish.' Mrs Gubbins lost her case, as the judge felt that she had misunderstood the terms on which she had been engaged to wash the surplice.

The hearing was widely reported, and it is not surprising that the editor of the *Secular Chronicle* made a scathing comment on the case in the edition which was printed on 28 March 1875. The secularist movement campaigned against the Church, which was seen by them as a privileged institution, and the editor of the *Secular Chronicle*, Harriet Law, was a prominent figure within the movement. This incident was an example of the atrocious behaviour they felt epitomised what was wrong with the Church, and the publication reported that, 'The Reverend Edward Muckleston, the Rector of Haseley, deserves the honour of the world for his steadfast adherence to principle. He will make no compromise with either "the world, the flesh, or the devil" – or his washerwoman.' They summarised the evidence given in court and finished by sarcastically saying, 'We congratulate MUCKLESTON on his triumphant vindication of principle at the expense of his washerwoman.'

In the same year, Edward took on fourteen-year-old Richard Morris as a servant. Young Richard was an inmate at the local workhouse and may have thought himself very fortunate to leave that inhospitable building in the polluted town centre to live and work in a large house in the fresher air of the countryside alongside a rector, his wife, daughter and housekeeper. Warwick Poor Law Union had been formed in 1836 and its operation was overseen by a board of guardians. Between 1837 and 1839 a union workhouse was built in Warwick and the guardians did their best to find positions for those who needed help and were unfortunate to find themselves within the building's grim, unwelcoming walls. The guardians, for their part, surely felt their duty done towards Richard, having placed him with a clergyman and his family, who would surely set a good example and give the right guidance to this poor pauper boy.

In September that year an inspector by the name of Mr Stephens visited the rectory intending to check on the boy's welfare, only to be turned away. Edward had refused to see the inspector and denied him access to the boy. Edward may have been caught unawares by the visit and wanted to speak to the boy to advise him what he should and should not say about what was going on during what was a turbulent time for the family. When Mr Stephens reported back to the board, they recommended that the boy should be called to attend the board meeting planned for a fortnight's time, if Stephens was not allowed access to him before then.[198] This incident had been reported in the local newspaper and as such, Edward was aware of the board's decision and it is most likely that he relented and allowed access to the boy at his home rather than allow him to be questioned out of sight.

It may have been that, now having a wife and child, Edward felt that Mary Ann needed additional help, or was she older than the census had indicated and, as she was ageing, finding it difficult to do the heavier work? Either way, her service came to an end when she passed away at the Warneford Hospital in Leamington Spa after ten years of service.[199] Although just five years earlier Edward had recorded her age as forty-three on the 1871 census, when he buried her at Haseley he entered her age as seventy years old in the register. When Mary Ann Blower's death was officially registered, probably by a member of her family who required a death certificate, her age was given as sixty-five. Even Mary Ann's burial led to controversy.

Henry Cook, a carpenter in Warwick, also acted as an undertaker, and when the decision was taken to bury Mary Ann in the parish in which she had spent the last ten years of her life, the task of arranging the funeral naturally fell to him. However, Mary Ann's brothers, Thomas and Richard Blower who lived in Shrewsbury, were not happy about the arrangements made, especially the cost of the funeral, and refused to pay the bill for £34-4s-6d [around £2,000 today] submitted to them. This amount included the sum of £18 [around £1,000 today], which Henry claimed to have advanced Mary Ann during her lifetime, the rest being funeral costs. Henry Cook arranged for the brothers to be summoned to Warwick County Court in front of Judge Harrington, where he explained that he knew Mary Ann very well and had assisted her with her investments. The investments were mainly deposited with the Warwick Building Society, where she was a regular investor between 1869 and her death, and there was a passbook in her name showing the savings. It is not made clear exactly how Mary came to owe Mr Cook £18, but he managed to convince the judge of the debt owed to him.

The funeral was another matter, as much of the expense had not been agreed. For example, new gloves had been purchased for the undertaker and rector (Edward) and billed to the next of kin, as had extensive refreshments, none of which had been requested by the family. Mary Ann's brothers, as her executors, had deposited £13-10s-0d [around £850 today] with the court, the amount they felt should be the true cost of the funeral. Judge Harrington had Henry Cook talk through the funeral expenses, stating that he could only claim what was absolutely necessary for the funeral. The judge ultimately agreed that the amount now held by the court was a fair amount, rather than the £16-4s-6d the executors had originally been billed, plus the monies owed to Henry, who was also granted the cost of bringing the case to court.[200] A small victory for the brothers, who now had Edward in their sights.

Early in 1877,[201] Edward was once again standing in the dock of the Warwick County Court House in front of Judge Harrington, on this occasion due to a summons brought against him by Mary Ann's executors, her brothers Richard and Thomas Blower. The case gave rise to sensational headlines in the local newspapers: 'The Rector of Haseley and his Housekeeper'[202] and 'Curious Action Against a Clergyman'[203] were just two. Mary Ann had apparently told her brothers that she was owed £50 in wages [about £3,200 today] at the time of her death, but Edward had denied owing her anything and was in court to prove it. The brothers set out to paint Edward in a poor light; they raised the fact about the loan which Mary Ann had made him and her losses as a result of the bankruptcy. There was also a dispute as to exactly how much she was paid; they believed £18 but Edward stated it was £16. He testified that Mary Ann had asked for £18, but he had only been able to afford £16 and she had accepted this. He said she had been a good woman and had been treated as a member of the family.

The brothers testified that at the time Edward was

made bankrupt, £4 was owed to their sister in wages and that it was entered in the documentation that she was paid £18 a year. When Edward was questioned why £18 was entered in his bankruptcy proceedings if she was not paid this amount, he claimed she had proved herself and he was unaware of what she had claimed, saying, 'She did it but without my authority.' When asked why he did not object when it was entered, he said, 'I took no notice of it.' When the judge challenged, 'You as a clergyman of the Church of England knowing she was committing perjury took no notice of it. You must have known she made affidavit of her proof,' Edward simply stated, 'I did not see it.' He confirmed she had always received £16 a year and that he had a memorandum book in which he entered all the sums of money he paid her and produced the book. It would not come as a surprise if Edward had encouraged Mary Ann to inflate her claim at the time of his bankruptcy, thus explaining the difference in her wage figure, and it makes you wonder if the amount she claimed to have loaned him was also true.

This book was duly inspected by the judge, jury and Mr Warren, who represented the brothers. A few of the entries in the ledger raised suspicions and Edward was challenged as to whether some of them were really made on the dates stated, to which he replied, 'Yes I will swear it, I have not made a mistake on any one of them.' One of the entries of concern occurred on 23 September of the previous year, which indicated that Mary Ann had received £10-10s-0d despite only being owed fourteen days' wages at the time. When this was queried, Edward's response was, 'I had money at the time.' Another question arose as to why, on 17 November, he had recorded two payments being made to his servant, one of £5 and another of £2, to which he responded, 'I cannot say why I made separate entries, I have no reason.' When questioned where Mary's money had gone, he replied, 'She spent very extravagantly amongst her relations and on one occasion she went to Shrewsbury, Liverpool and other places.' He went on to say, 'She went visiting her relations in June 1874 I believe. She stayed away about a month and took a great deal of money with her.' Edward was asked by the plaintiff's counsel if she had gone to her brothers at Shrewsbury, to which he replied, 'I did not go with her you know,' and the counsel queried, 'No you would not like to go to Shrewsbury?' Edward responded that, 'I have done nothing to be ashamed of,' to which the judge, no doubt referring to the well-known fare-dodging charges, said, 'Nothing to be ashamed of?' to which Edward replied, 'Not at Shrewsbury.'

The stamps within the books also appeared to be out of order, as there were old stamps against some of the more recent entries. His honour called attention to other entries in the book and asked if these were advances to the deceased, and Edward confirmed that they were. He went on to state that he had charged her five per cent interest as she wanted the money to invest in other securities. As Mary Ann was illiterate, he explained she had simply made the mark of a X when she received the money.

In summing up, Mr Warren addressed the jury and declared that the memorandum book entries clearly showed that the books had been 'cooked' to enable Edward to avoid paying outstanding wages to Mary Ann's executors, and instead of Edward lending his servant money, that it had been the other way around. He also asked the jury if they really believed that Reverend Muckleston, or anyone else for that matter, really paid their servants in advance and if they did not believe that the wages had been paid in advance, then there was money owed up to the end of the year. He also made the point that the statement of the deceased in the bankruptcy proceedings also evidenced that she was paid £18 a year, which was different to that testified by the defendant during the current proceedings.

Edward's counsel then turned to the jury and stated that Mary Ann's executors were not suing for loans made, but for wages, and this was simply a speculative action brought against Edward out of spite and that the wages had all been paid up. There was also no evidence that the defendant had ever seen the proof for £18 which the deceased had made at the time of his bankruptcy.

Sitting in his chair overlooking the court, Judge Harrington turned to the jury and instructed them that the proof of payment was upon the party by whom payment was alleged to have been made. The jury must not allow themselves to be influenced by any rumours affecting the credit of Mr Muckleston, as they were not proved in this case, although it was perfectly competent for the plaintiffs to have called witnesses to show that the defendant's word could not be relied upon. He went on to say that it was an extraordinary thing that directly after his bankruptcy Edward alleged that he paid the deceased £5 for wages and £5 for a loan. It was worthy of notice too that entries professed to have been made in 1869 had the modern receipt stamps, whilst those made later had old receipt stamps. If the modern receipt stamps were not available in 1869, which had not been proven, then the entries could not have been made then; however it was not impossible for some old receipt stamps to be found in a drawer and used up. Surely, much to his relief, the jury, having been locked up for some time, found for Edward and the case against him was dismissed.[204]

The brothers were tenacious, and two months later, partly inspired by the length of time it had taken the jury to come to a decision, which probably indicated that they had doubts, they returned to the Warwick County Court to request a new trial. Their argument was that they had examined papers at Shrewsbury and Sheffield, and now had evidence that Edward had signed a statement declaring that the particulars regarding the bankruptcy proceedings were true.[205] Rather damningly, this included an entry for Mary Ann's wages in Edward's own handwriting, and they could now prove that Edward had sworn on oath to two different statements regarding the amount his servant was paid. His honour asked why they had not asked for an adjournment of the previous case if they thought new evidence would be forthcoming, as if this had then been refused then there would have been grounds for a new trial. The judge advised that if they felt that Edward had committed perjury then they should press for such a case. He did not think, however, that there was enough alleged to justify him in granting a new trial, saying that, 'If new trials were granted on these grounds then there would never be an end to litigation.' He did, however, feel that if Edward was to be found guilty of perjury in a criminal case then there could well be grounds for a new trial on that basis.[206]

On reading this in the local newspaper, Edward would surely have been worried that his next visit to court would be a more serious one. A criminal conviction would likely lead to time in prison and that would certainly be something the bishop could not ignore. Edward's usual method of dealing with these situations was to offer money to make the problem go away and, as there is no evidence that the Blower brothers sought to obtain a perjury charge against Edward, they may have used the possibility to persuade him to settle out of court.

Despite the ill feeling between Edward and her relatives, he placed a marker on Mary Ann's grave, although he did make it quite clear that he had done so by having the words, 'Mary Blower obit 1876 at 70 yrs. Erected by Rev. E. Muckleston in memory of her faithful service.'

Following Mary Ann's death there was quite a turnover of servants at the rectory, and in late 1880 Edward and Emily were looking for a new housemaid. Ellen Rawlings applied for the post, was interviewed and offered the position which she accepted. They had agreed on a salary of £8 per annum [approximately £530 today] plus board,

Mary Ann Blower's grave marker at Haseley.

starting on 24 November. During the negotiations Edward had seen her several times, and she visited the vicarage and confirmed that she would be starting work for the couple. Ellen failed to take up the post and, on the day she was due to start, a letter was sent saying she would not be taking up the position. She had found better employment elsewhere and this caused inconvenience for the family, who had to employ more expensive temporary help until another permanent housemaid could be found.

Clearly annoyed by Ellen's actions, Edward once again turned to the court in Warwick,[207] but this time as the plaintiff. He was suing Ellen for the sum of 13s-4d damages sustained in consequence of her non-compliance with the terms of contract and as a result losing the opportunity to engage another servant. During the hearing Edward was asked how long he had employed a temporary employee, to which he responded, 'About a month at the rate of one shilling a day plus board.' His answer was too vague for the judge, who pressed him to be more accurate, asking if it was really a month and to how long would he be prepared to swear he had employed the temporary servant. Being pressed in such a manner, Edward admitted it had been a fortnight.

The judge was certain that there was proof of a contract between the rector and Ellen Rawlings, and that she had declined to fulfil her part of it. He went on to say that he was not sorry Edward had brought this action, as he wanted it publicly understood that anyone who entered into engagements as domestic servants, were no more able to break their contracts than other persons. In the present case, however, Reverend Muckleston was not entitled to recover the sum of 13s-4d, a month's wages, because the contract was never entered into and he had no right to a month's wages which had never been begun. If the defendant had actually entered into the service of the plaintiff, as a servant, the case would have been different. He went on to say that Edward appeared to have paid the sum of 14 shillings [around £44 today] for the services of another woman to take the place of the defendant, and was therefore entitled to the difference between the 6s-8d he would have had to pay to Ellen and the 14s-0d he was obliged to pay, which was 7s-4d, but inasmuch as half a calendar month was probably over a fortnight he should give judgment for 7s-0d [around £22 today], which would be 'sufficient for all practical purposes'. Ellen was required to make the payment within fourteen days.[208] Yet another person who had cause to regret the day they crossed paths with the Reverend Muckleston and another petty win for Edward.

Edward had a second case in Warwick County Court that same day and, no doubt buoyed up by his earlier success, was looking for another positive outcome, although this case was a little more complicated. Mr W. S. Dorsett, a gentleman farmer, had been renting the sixty-seven-acre Glebe Farm from Edward, but when his tenancy came to an end, in March 1880, there was a dispute over money owed under the Agricultural Holdings Act and arbitrators had been brought in. The final decision was that Edward owed Mr Dorsett £158-0s-5d [around £10,500 today], but he did not have the means to pay this amount at the time. It was therefore agreed that Mr Dorsett would remain on the farm as a day tenant rent-free, using the buildings, to have grazing rights and a certain acreage until the award was paid to him, or the benefit he gained from remaining at the property equalled that which was owed to him. It was anticipated that Mr Dorsett would remain under these conditions until 23 May, whilst the rest of the farm reverted to Edward. During this temporary tenancy a quantity of manure was made, and the dispute was brought to court over whether this manure belonged to Mr Dorsett or his landlord. Edward claimed it should be his and, as Mr Dorsett had taken away the manure, he was suing him for the sum of £9 [around £600 today], the value of the manure.

Mr Whittingdale, the arbitrator, was called as a witness. Edward's contention was that Mr Dorsett only had the right of grazing cattle at six pence a head and that the manure in the yard was not part of the agreement and belonged to the landlord. Mr Whittingdale confirmed that when drawing up the agreement, the question of manure had never occurred to him. His honour then delivered judgment at some length and said in the present case there must be a non-suit, but it was desirable that he explained his decision. He held that 'the customs of the ordinary agricultural tenancy did not apply to this particular arrangement. The manure was just as much the property of the defendant as if it was made by horses in a stable which he rented. Looking into the whole circumstances of the case there must be a non-suit'. Mr Dorsett applied for costs, which his honour granted.[209]

Edward's day in court as a plaintiff in these two cases had therefore been an expensive one; the cost of bringing the claim against Mr Dorsett would far outweigh the nine shillings from poor Ellen Rawlings.

Despite the adverse publicity surrounding the family in the newspapers, the rural location of the rectory and undoubtedly wages on the lower side of what would be expected, servants did not seem to be in short supply. In 1881,[210] when the national census was taken in England, Edward and Emily were employing two live-in domestic servants, plus a man and a boy to work on the farm. Twenty-year-old Jane E. Robinson from Shipston-upon-Stour in Worcestershire and fifteen-year-old Agnes M. Brasbridge from Barford, situated six miles south of Haseley, were employed as general servants to keep the house clean and carry out other tasks which would have enabled Emily to take care of her two children.[211]

As a bachelor, Edward had preferred a single more mature servant to care for him. As mistress of the house, Emily was responsible for interviewing and deciding upon the servants, and it appears that she preferred them younger and less experienced. As a young woman herself, she may have found it difficult to command an older woman. Many employers did not like their servants to come from the immediate locality, as they may have gossiped about the family and betrayed their secrets, and it is, therefore, not surprising that the two female servants employed at this time came from some distance away. Having a distance to travel, it was also less likely that the younger servants would run back home, and as they were expected to live in, they also needed to be single. It was not unusual for a servant who planned to marry or became pregnant to be asked to leave. Whilst in service they would learn how to run a home and they would find the standards vastly different to those encountered in the poverty-stricken, overcrowded homes they had come from. In some cases, they may not even have known the names of the pieces of furniture they were expected to clean. As general servants they were expected to carry out the duties of the plethora of servants, from cook to scullery maid, employed in the wealthier homes.

On 6 November 1881 Jane would marry Francis Pinfold, a labourer who was related to Cornelius Pinfold, Edward's bailiff. This was just one of the problems that came from employing young servants. They chose not to marry at Haseley; instead they were married at nearby Hatton by the vicar of that parish.

As well as their regular servants, there was a requirement for additional help from time to time, and one such employment would once again see Edward standing in the dock at Warwick County Court defending his actions.

Henry Edwards of Brook Street, Warwick had been employed by Edward to hoe five acres of wheat. They had agreed on the payment of £1 [about £65 today] for the work and Edward paid ten shillings on account. When the work was finished, he applied to Edward for the outstanding amount, only for his request to be refused as Edward did not think that the work had been completed to the required standard. Henry decided that his only recourse was to take him to court.

Once again standing in the dock in front of the now 'Sir' Richard Harrington, who could surely only wonder how many times the reverend gentleman was going to appear before him, Edward once again felt right was on his side. When called to give evidence, Henry said that he did not agree to clear the land of weeds but to hoe the wheat, and had he turned up all the weeds he would also have hoed up the corn. He agreed that there might be some thistles left that were higher than the wheat. He was supported by witness, Charles King of Friar's Street, Warwick, another labourer, who said that the night before the work was finished, he walked over the field and he considered that it was done as well as Henry was able to do it. Clearly annoyed, Judge Harrington cut the case short and dismissed the charge, adding that if he was wrong it was because 'persons were foolish enough to bring before a lawyer a matter which should have been decided better by a practical farmer.'[212]

In August 1885, Emily was advertising for help once more:[213]

WANTED, steady General Servant, for Lady and Gentleman, in quiet place.—Particulars, apply, Mrs. MUCKLESTON, Hasely, Warwick.

Edward would however be responsible for any male servants and those required to work on the land, and nine months after Emily's advertisement they were looking for more help:[214]

WANTED, an experienced Gardener, married or single, who understands the management of greenhouse and vinery, lawn, and kitchen garden, and who has had some experience with management of milking cows; there is a boy kept to help.—Apply to Rev. EDWARD MUCKLESTON, Hasely Rectory, Warwick.

The boy 'kept to help' mentioned in the advert was almost certainly another boy from a workhouse, but a few years later Edward's preference for this source of servants was to lead to major trouble for the reverend, and his poor attitude towards those he employed was again to be made public.

Chapter Fourteen

The Derailing of Reverend Muckleston

THE DEW WAS HEAVY ON THE GRASS AS EDWARD left the rectory at Haseley and it was to be yet another momentous day in his extraordinary life. It was early on the morning of Thursday 6 May 1875, and the weather was fine and clear with occasional glimpses of sunshine.[215] The rolling rural landscape was busy with farmers and farmhands, who had already been at work for several hours. An indefatigable walker, in his stout boots Edward made light work of the seven-mile journey across the Warwickshire countryside; arriving at Knowle railway station shortly before nine in the morning, he purchased a third-class railway ticket from Thomas Parsons the station master. The ticket was a single to Hatton, the nearest railway station to his home and next on the line to Knowle, but he did not immediately use it. Edward was to later say that, at Knowle, he met a gentleman farmer in his carriage and obtained a lift to Small Heath, a suburb of Birmingham, which was a city some twenty miles to the north of Haseley. When asked, he declined to name this man, saying that he did not want to get him into trouble.

During his time in Birmingham, Edward made several purchases and, to avoid carrying them, he asked the various tradespersons to arrange for the packages to be delivered to the first-class waiting room at Snow Hill railway station, at that time the main station in the centre of Birmingham, to await his collection later in the day. Edward was fully aware that, ever since his conviction eight years earlier, he was regularly watched by the police inspectors working for the Great Western Railway, but maybe, since he had not used the railway that day, did not think to check if he was being followed on this occasion. Possibly alerted by the parcels arriving at the station, Railway Police Inspector John Ledbrooke became aware that Edward was in the vicinity and would later testify that he watched him the whole of the afternoon endeavouring to identify which train he planned to travel by.

It had been a long and busy day for Edward when he arrived at the station shortly before the last train left at ten past eleven. Snow Hill had been rebuilt in 1871 as a solid brick structure with two through platforms, and its arched roof provided Edward with some protection from the cool night air.[216] He found that there was no porter available to help and so consequently had to move the parcels from the waiting room to the platform himself. When the train arrived, the parcels were stowed in the baggage car and Edward took his seat in a third-class carriage. This activity had been observed by Ledbrooke, who noted that no attempt had been made to purchase a ticket and Edward was completely unaware that the inspector had also joined the same train. Due to the darkness, there was little to see as the train trundled along on the eighteen-mile journey south, picking up and dropping off the last of the day's passengers at the local stations along the way.

Edward was the only passenger to alight at Hatton and his boy was there to meet him and to take charge of removing his master's parcels from the train. Meanwhile the station's ticket collector, Joseph William Shaw, approached Edward and, on checking the ticket, said, 'From Knowle to Hatton Sir,' and he replied, 'Yes Shaw. I came up by the short train.' He had handed over the ticket purchased that morning. During a five-minute conversation, Shaw went on to explain that Edward's 'boy' had arrived at the station at around ten o'clock, and the staff had shared their supper and ale with him and allowed him to sleep on the bench whilst he waited for his master. Edward dug into his pocket and pulled out a threepenny bit and offered it to Shaw for his trouble; Shaw was initially reluctant to take the money, but he was pressed and ultimately accepted it. The boy then gathered up his master's purchases and they left the station, setting out to walk the mile home. Ledbrooke had also left the train at Hatton, unnoticed by Edward.

Having observed the exchange between Edward and the ticket collector, Inspector Ledbrooke approached Shaw and asked him to recount the conversation and show him the ticket that had been handed over. In consequence, he then hurriedly left the station, heading along the lane after the departing pair and called out to the reverend gentleman and asked him if he knew who he was. Edward confirmed that he did and asked how he could assist him, at which point they were asked to return to the station. Ledbrooke enquired as to what ticket Edward had given up and he confirmed it was a ticket from Knowle to Hatton. When asked if he felt that it was the proper ticket to give up, he answered, 'No I suppose not but I did not have time to take a ticket at Birmingham,' and then he went on to explain that, due to the fact that he had to do his own porterage at Snow Hill, he did not have time to purchase a ticket before boarding the train. Edward told him that if anything was wrong he would make it right, and he had travelled on the line every fortnight for about six years, never making a mistake. Edward then pressed the police inspector to take whatever payment was due, saying that Ledbrooke had ruined him once and would ruin him again. The inspector refused to take any payment, stating that he would have to report the matter as an act of fraud.

Edward's wife Emily, four months pregnant, was at home with two-year-old daughter Mabel, and we can only wonder at her reaction when he recounted the events of the day. Edward's character was again being called into account and, once again, the local gossip was all about the Rector of Haseley. Shortly after his encounter Edward received a summons to appear at Solihull Police Court on Saturday 5 June to answer a charge of fraud. The town of Solihull, three miles south-east of Knowle, had a petty sessions court from the end of the eighteenth century and also its own county court. Whether Edward could not find a solicitor prepared to act for him, did not have the financial means to pay for a representative or simply thought that he knew enough about the law to represent himself, we cannot know, but he decided to conduct his own defence.

With the move towards professionalising the police force, a system of paid magistrates had been established in police offices. It was the decision of the two or three magistrates sitting at these police courts to decide whether to send those who appeared before them either to the House of Correction (limited to three months with hard labour), or to be sent to appear at the Quarter Sessions, or to decide how to punish the offender locally. The magistrates sitting at Solihull on this Saturday were Messers H. H. Chattock and G. A. Everitt. The charge against Edward was 'defrauding the Great Western Railway Company, by travelling on their line from Birmingham to Knowle, without paying his fare on 6th May'. Mr Lee, of the firm Whateley and Milward, appeared for the prosecution.

Mr Lee opened the case by saying that he regretted to appear against a gentleman of the defendant's profession, but the railway company felt bound to take up the case, as this was not the first time the defendant had committed such an offence and because it was absolutely necessary to prevent such an offence being carried out by other persons. He went on to outline the events of the day and said that he appreciated that he had to prove intent to defraud and believed he would do so. He stated that Edward had given first one story to the ticket collector at Hatton and then another to the police inspector shortly after, and then did everything he could to compromise the case by offering Ledbrooke payment. He called as witnesses Thomas Parsons, station master at Knowle; Joseph William Shaw, ticket collector at Hatton Station; and John Ledbrooke, police inspector. All three witnesses recounted the events of the day. John Ledbrooke was to say that Edward arrived at Snow Hill a good five minutes before the last train and he believed with enough time to purchase a ticket. Mr Chattock asked Ledbrooke if Edward had been convicted before and he said, 'Yes at Oswestry in 1867 and two other cases were compromised.' Mr Lee said that this was the reason they followed him as they did.

In conducting his own defence, Edward firstly recalled Joseph Shaw and asked if he had given him tickets over the last six years, and the ticket collector confirmed that he had indeed given him tickets but could not confirm for how long, nor could he say if they were correct or not. Edward asked him if he had ever known him to make a mistake in all that time. Shaw stated none that he was aware of but went on to say, 'I recollect once you made the mistake of getting out of a second-class carriage with a third-class ticket and I got 10 ½d from you.' Edward said he could not remember that incident, to which Shaw replied, 'You had the goodness to write to Mr Andrews to know whether we paid it into the office or not.'

Edward had no witnesses to call but took to the box himself, where he reiterated that he did not have time to purchase a ticket at Birmingham due to having to undertake his own porterage and that the inspector was always trying to injure him. He had known Ledbrooke watch him several times in the streets of Birmingham, he had put reports about against him and he never could leave him alone, as he was always doing something to injure him. He was glad that he had come to court to explain the case and whilst he had no solicitor to defend him, he hoped the bench would consider his word as good as the inspector's. They were paid for their work and he dare say the officials were primed by their excellent solicitor to make these remarks against him. He said that he had no more idea of committing a fraud for the sake of 9d [approximately £4 today] and getting him into this 'scrape' than he had of flying. He had paid pounds to the GWR and reiterated that he had not made a mistake for six years. The clerk, a Mr Mitchell, advised Edward that he should not make these charges and pointed out that he had the opportunity to recall the witnesses should he wish to do so, but Edward declined.

Mr Everitt said it seemed extraordinary that the defendant should go from Haseley to Knowle so early in the morning and take a ticket under the circumstances given in the evidence, and then go on to Birmingham, to which Edward stated that he often walked from Haseley to Knowle. After a short consultation, the magistrates found him guilty of fraud and fined him forty shillings plus costs, a total of £3-17s-4 ½ d [approximately £400 today], which was the highest penalty they could impose.[217]

The court cases concerning Edward regularly featured in the *Leamington Spa Courier* and, having been made aware of the new difficulties facing the reverend gentleman, they ensured that their reporter was in court to enable them to share the full details of the case with their readers. The fraud case was also reported nationally but, fortunately for Edward, only warranted a few lines, as at the same time there was a scandalous case against another clergyman, 'The Reverend T. M. Hughes whose vagaries at Beaumaris have brought his name into such unfortunate notoriety, was on Saturday sentenced to three months' imprisonment for being drunk and assaulting his step daughter and other persons.'[218]

Harriet Shaw, still editor of the *Secular Chronicle*, who had lampooned Edward earlier in the year following the case concerning his washerwoman, also picked up on this conviction and reported, 'The Rev. Edward Muckleston has had to pay £3-17s-4 ½ d for defrauding the Great Western Railway company of 9d. He had been convicted once before for a similar offence. The reverend swindler should praise God that he has not been locked up in durance vile [*received a very long prison sentence].'*[219] Edward was indeed lucky to have, once again, avoided a more serious punishment. For the next couple of months Edward's clerical duties were covered by Reverend Frederick Stonehouse, the vicar of nearby Honiley, although whether this was by Edward's request to allow the controversy to dissipate or that of Bishop Philpott is not clear. There is nothing in the bishop's papers relating to disciplinary matters regarding the situation at Haseley, although, at that time, he was possibly preoccupied in dealing with another vicar who had fathered an illegitimate child.

Chapter Fifteen

Conflict with the Corporation

EDWARD'S CONFLICTS WITH OTHERS WERE NOT JUST dealt with through the courts. For an eight-year period from 1876 through to 1884, his name constantly appeared in the minutes of the meetings held by the local corporation. The corporation, or town council, was a group of local people who made decisions relating to many areas of civic administration, much like the local councils do in England today. As with the railways, Edward seems to have had an ongoing grievance against them, starting in January 1876 when Edward applied for a summons against a Mr Charles Pratt, the highway surveyor for the parish of Budbrooke. Edward complained that the hedges of the highway between Warwick and Hatton, a regular walking route of his, were sixteen foot high in places, and portions projected and overhung to an inconvenient extent. On walking past them, he had his clothes torn and his face scratched. Edward was asked if he had spoken to the surveyor on the matter and he responded by saying that he had not received a reply to a letter that he had sent. The court declined his request, advising Edward that it was down to the surveyor to take proceedings against the owner of the hedges should he deem it necessary.[220]

However, Edward's longest-running grievance against the Warwick Town Council came from the fact that the Mill Pool at Haseley supplied the water for the town of Warwick and it was situated next to glebe land. Near to the Glebe Farm, 500 yards north of the church, stood a watermill fed by a rivulet called Inchford Brook, a small clear waterway running through the parish. There had been a mill on this site since before 1086 and records show two watermills in 1632. When he had first arrived in the parish, there was a was a mill pond bordering Edward's property which caused him no issues. In 1872 this was all to change when the government passed the Warwick Waterworks Act, which had been obtained to supply the town of Warwick with a clean water supply. Since 1857 the townspeople of Warwick had taken their water from the Avon; towns such as Leamington and Coventry further up the river were allowing their sewerage to discharge into the waterway and it was described as scandalously filthy. The source of this new water supply was to be the small stream running through Haseley, with the engineers believing that, as there had been a mill on the site for over 800 years, there would be a good constant water supply.

Tests were undertaken, the flow of water was measured, and eleven acres of land were purchased from Frederick Hewlett at a cost of £2,250 [about a quarter of a million pounds today] which was to house the two reservoirs. Water was then to be run through pipes by gravitation down to the town and the whole project was expected to cost £17,500 [the equivalent of £2 million pounds today]. As the engineers started work on the project and were studying the flow of the water, it became apparent that there was another source feeding into the brook and an underground reservoir was discovered. It was anticipated that this new source could supply 240,000 gallons of water a day to the town. Although the surface water storage was no longer needed, the method of getting water to the town remained the same, and adits (a form of tunnel) were cut to access the supply.[221]

The project took two years to complete and the water was deemed to be of excellent quality. No doubt during that time Edward had tolerated the workers and their equipment passing the rectory daily. The expected cost had been exceeded, and there was an enquiry into this, but then so had the supply, as 500,000 gallons of water a day could now be supplied to the town, much more than required. The corporation also owned the acres of land which they had purchased for the reservoirs, which were no longer required, and they were now free to sell or dispose of this land as they wished. There was a grand opening of the water supply on Tuesday 26 September 1876, with the

Haseley Water Mill after its closure (photograph circa 1950s).

mayor and councillors from the town visiting the site, and the bells of St Mary's rang out in celebration. Little more than a year later Edward had started an ongoing complaint to the councillors of Warwick looking for compensation due to the water from the waterworks flooding the glebe land and making it impossible to farm a portion of it.

In May 1878 Edward's solicitor, a Mr W. B. Sanderson, wrote to the corporation on his behalf, stating that valuable meadows on the glebe land had been damaged by water and had become worthless for mowing. He went on to say that water from the pool was so pounded up that it backs up and chokes and fills the drainpipes upon Edward's land. This meant that the drainage from his farm could not run into the brook as it had done before the waterworks had been constructed and the problem was becoming worse every year. He also had another complaint in that the corporation had not fulfilled their undertaking to clay up the bank of the pool which had now given way owing to want of care. He went on to say that if they did not show a disposition to meet him fairly, legal proceedings would commence.[222] His complaint was referred to the Waterworks Committee.

Clearly nothing happened, as in November 1878 Mr Sanderson was once more writing to the corporation regarding the problems the waterworks were causing his client and looking for payment of damages and assurances that steps would be taken to keep the Mill Pool at a lower level to avoid ongoing damage. In the letter referring to Edward he included the line 'I have no wonder that his patience is exhausted', to which one of the councillors commented 'Is it his patience or his pocket that is exhausted?'. The solicitor went on to say that Edward had instructed him to issue a writ against the corporation for damages; and to apply for an injunction in respect to the water in the Mill Pool unless the corporation took immediate steps to comply with the demands made upon them. Once again it was proposed by the council members to send the letter to the Waterworks Committee.[223]

At the next council meeting in December the Waterworks Committee reported that, with reference to the Mill Pool at Haseley, the level of the water had been permanently lowered since the mill was purchased by the corporation, and was now considerably lower than the height to which the miller had the right of keeping it; the committee was of the opinion that no case of damage to Mr Muckleston's land had occurred and that his claim should therefore be resisted and the councillors agreed to this course of action.[224]

Edward, however, was not going to give up on his claim and Mr Sanderson once again wrote to the corporation.[225]

Dear Sir,
    Muckleston v Corporation.

Fortified by the opinion of an eminent counsel I am now in the position to institute the proceedings which have been previously threatened by my client for the injury and damage done to his glebe land. Before however taking such proceedings and seeing that the proceedings would in all probability result in a reference to arbitration, I am willing to submit the question of compensation for injury done to the arbitrament of any competent practical referee, or I am willing to say what sum my client will feel justified in asking the corporation to pay him. Any such reference would be entirely outside and independent of his right to apply for an injunction to restrain the corporation from causing or continuing to cause the water of the mill dam to be pounded up to the injury of his land. Already the new tenant of the glebe land, which I am glad to say he has at length found a tenant, but at a very reduced rental, has complained about the pounding up of the mill dam to his injury, and it is a positive fact for the last three weeks or thereabouts the water has been pounded up to the utmost height, and the attention of your surveyor has been called to this. This I apprehend is clearly a matter for an injunction and is easy of proof. Favour me with a reply at your earliest opportunity.

I am Dear Sir,
Yours faithfully,
W B Sanderson.

Once again, the letter was referred to the Waterworks Committee and at their meeting held on 26 June, the committee reported that 'with regards to the Haseley Waterworks, they had considered the letters from Mr Sanderson of the 7th and 24th ult., relative to the claim of the Reverend E. Muckleston, and recommended that the council adhere to the view expressed in their report of the 29 November last', and they declined to refer the situation to arbitration, considering it would be questioning the undoubted right of the council to back up the water.[226]

There is no evidence that Edward carried out his threat to take proceedings against the Warwick Corporation, but some five years later, according to the town council minutes of July 1884, he appears to have taken matters into his own hands and it was alleged that he had 'unlawfully extracted water from the Haseley pool'.[227] The Waterworks Committee recommended that the council authorise the town clerk to take any proceedings necessary against Edward as quickly as possible. The minutes of the August meeting indicate that there was insufficient evidence to proceed against him and it was reported, 'The question of the Reverend Muckleston having taken the corporation water at Haseley has been several times mentioned to him lately. He [*Mr W Smith, the clerk*] regretted that the evidence had been deemed to be insufficient to take proceedings against the reverend gentleman and he would certainly not like it to be thought that Mr Muckleston was at perfect liberty to use the water in future. If he did so again, he hoped it would be understood that a prosecution would be instituted.' The mayor advised the clerk that on looking at all the evidence, they did think it was insufficient to proceed against him, but they had warned Mr Muckleston what would happen if he took further water.

Having tried to take matters in to his own hands by reducing the water levels himself to avoid damage to his land, Edward returned to resorting to solicitor letters, and once again Mr Sanderson was asked to write to the corporation requesting that action be taken regarding the level of the water in the Mill Pool. At their April meeting in 1885, the Waterworks Committee once again stated that, 'we would not recommend that any concession be made to Mr Muckleston'. The committee explained that the mill premises were purchased from Messers Ball in 1876 and there was no question that not only had the council the power to keep the water at the present level but to raise it considerably higher and it would be unwise to abandon any water rights attached to the ownership of Haseley Mill, as it might be necessary to raise the water level to its original level in the future.[228] The members of the council unanimously agreed that they would not give any concession to Edward. Never one to give up, Edward put in a further claim for damage done to his crops by reason of floods during the spring and summer of 1888, but once again the council repudiated any liability.[229]

Besides the issue with the Mill Pool, Edward was also a regular complainant about the local environment, and in 1891 he wrote to the Kenilworth Highways Committee asking them to widen the bridge over the brook in Roundsill Lane. They replied stating that they were under no obligation to do so and they did not consider it expedient to carry out any work on the bridge at the present time.[230]

In October 1897 it was reported that Edward had written to the surveyor for the Warwick Rural District Council complaining that a footpath running through parts of Hatton and Shrewley had been closed a few years ago by the late Mr Bell. He was the owner of the land through which the footpath led and was closed due to 'trippers' from Birmingham trespassing upon his grass. Edward felt that if the path was reopened and repaired it would be a great convenience to the public as an approach to the railway station. It was argued that the path was never a public footpath, it was not on the map, and from information gathered, the path was originally for the accessibility of customers to 'a certain public house'. It was decided that the path would be of no convenience if it were opened.[231] Edward was an indefatigable walker and it was probably more for his own convenience rather than anyone else's that he felt this footpath, near to the station, should have been reopened to the public.

Edward's conflicts with the corporation were almost certainly financially motivated but another method he chose to save money would bring his name into serious disrepute.

Chapter Sixteen

The Shaming of Reverend Muckleston

B Y THE YEAR 1889, EDWARD WAS CASTING HIS NET wider for his boy servants and, to this end, approached the Board of Guardians at Alcester some thirteen miles south-west of Haseley. There were fifteen workhouses in Warwickshire, including those in the cities of Birmingham and Coventry, and they were a ready source of servants to the middle classes. On 29 June of that year it was entered in the minute book that the master of the workhouse had recommended Alfred Houghton, aged thirteen, to the Reverend Edward Muckleston to fulfil the position of page. Edward asked for the boy to be sent to him for a month on trial and the board agreed to purchase an outfit for Alfred before sending him off to Haseley.[232]

Those who could not support themselves found themselves in the workhouse. They were the poor, sick or old and some unmarried mothers who had been disowned by their families. Entry to a workhouse was voluntary and not a decision taken lightly. An interview enquiring into the personal circumstances of the applicants took place and agreement to take them would need the formal approval of the board of guardians at their weekly meetings. Inmates were initially stripped, bathed and issued with a workhouse uniform, their own clothes being disinfected and stored alongside any other belongings, to be returned when they left the institution. A government report in 1861 found that twenty per cent of the residents of the workhouses had been there for more than five years, but these were mainly the elderly, mentally ill and disabled. The survey also indicated that fifteen inmates had been residents for sixty years or more. Husbands, wives and older children were often separated on admission, the children under the age of seven usually remaining with their mother.

The workhouses were mainly self-sufficient and often had their own bakery, vegetable gardens, orchards and piggeries, as well as a shoemaker and tailor. There would have been a communal dining room, often with a dividing screen to separate the men and women, as well as workshops, a chapel and a schoolroom. The infirmary catered for the sick and there would usually be a separate fever ward, plus a mortuary, and, for a proportion of the inmates, this would be their last residence. Toilets were usually a simple privy, a cesspit with a board over it and a hole where they sat, often used by a hundred or more inmates. Those able to work were expected to clean, work in the kitchen, laundry or gardens and generally assist with the tasks involved in the running of the workhouse. In some rural areas, inmates could be set to work as agricultural labourers and religion would also play a part in daily life, including regular prayers.

The 1834 Poor Law Act stipulated that children should receive at least three hours' instruction a day in the subjects of reading, writing, arithmetic and the principles of Christianity. By the 1870s many poor law unions had set up district schools to educate the poor and the board of guardians often made use of these establishments to educate the children residing at the workhouse. As well as basic education, there were other lessons which would 'make them fit for service and train them to habits of usefulness, industry and virtue'.[233]

Alfred's mother was thirty-four-year-old Harriet Houghton, a charwoman from Bidford, who had given birth to her son in 1876 and had him baptised in that parish on 16 July 1876 and, as he was illegitimate, no father's name was entered in the baptism register. By 1881 she was in Alcester workhouse with her four-year-old son.

The matron took Alfred to meet Edward at Bearley Station where terms were agreed, those being that he would go to Haseley 'on trial' for a period of three months, during which time Edward would give him board, lodgings and clothe him. After the trial period, should he prove suitable, he would receive pay at the rate of £6 or £8 a year [around £500 or £650 today]. Alfred left his mother behind, but the prospect of work in a respectable house away from the harsh life of the workhouse and the opportunity to earn money was not to be missed. From Edward's perspective he had a 'boy' who would cost him very little for three months and someone that he could train to work in the way that he required. Everything appeared to have gone well during the trial period, at least the workhouse heard nothing to the contrary, but nine months after taking Alfred, Edward found it necessary to write to the master of Alcester workhouse.[234]

Haseley Rectory Warwick
Friday April 24th 1890

Dear Sir,

I regret much to tell you that the Alfred boy you sent me has turned out very bad. I fear he had got into bad company or had bad advice. I cannot keep him. I had to reprimand him for his idleness this morning, when actually he shook his fist in my face. Now such behaviour is not to be endured by him or any boy. I fear our servant girl has spoilt him. She is always pampering him. Will you name a day for me to send him back to you, or will you send somebody for him, the sooner he leaves here the better for me, as he is no use to me. He will not do his work and he idles about all the day long. If you have a nice deposed little boy, who you think would suit me, I will take him, but he must be a civil boy, and not like the one you are about to take back. I hope this will find you and your wife quite well.

I remain,
Yours truly,
Edw. Muckleston

P.S. A reply by return will greatly oblige me I have, owing to her conduct with the boy, given her notice to leave. If you know of a nice respectable woman who wants a place, Mrs Muckleston says if you will recommend her, she will take her upon your recommendation. Do you think that an old man out of the workhouse would suit me; there is less trouble with a man than a boy; the fact of poverty has made them humble minded.

The reverend and his wife were having issues with their servants, but we can only imagine what the master thought of Edward wanting someone who was humble-minded. Soon after the master received this letter from Edward, Alfred's mother, Harriet Houghton, had one from her son. She was still resident in the workhouse and so may have already had an inkling of what was in it. Alfred explained his version of events thus:

Haseley Rectory
27/04/90

My Dear Mother,

I now take the liberty of writing again to you. It is about my money. The master wanted to send me away on Friday last, but I told him I should not go till he gave me my money. He then said he should not. He has not said anything to me since then, nor do I want him to. He is known for about twenty miles around. He wanted to send me away because I would not let him hit me. He has hit me two or three times before with a spud, if you know what that is. It is an iron bar with a little wooden handle. He hit me two strokes across the back down at the farm, and one stroke on the head up here. He then hit me upstairs with his hands on my face. I do not like the place half as well, for he is such a nasty man. The missus one day says we eat too much bread and another day she says we don't eat enough. So here I must conclude, and,

I remain,
Your affectionate son,
Alfred Houghton

P.S. Will you please tell the matron about this, for it is right that she should know.

Physical chastisement of servants was common in Victorian times and, to write such a letter, Alfred was clearly intelligent and well educated. At the next board meeting both letters were discussed and the board heard that, after the boy had been at Haseley for three months and consequently became entitled to wages, the reverend gentleman began to discover that 'he didn't suit' and so he commenced 'amusing' himself by writing letters to the master making the most ridiculous and trivial complaints, all of which were denied point blank by the boy, who, by the end of May, had been sent back to the union. Mr Gothard, the clerk, investigated the situation and he soon learnt that Edward had similar transactions with other workhouses which he considered far from credible and concluded that, 'the only inference which I feel can be drawn from the extraordinary large number of pauper boys he has tried from the different unions, is that he desires to have his servants on the cheap'. From all the facts elicited during their meeting, the board felt that the boy's version was mostly likely to be the truer one. They were not to be trifled with and decided to demand the wages due to Alfred Houghton and that, 'they will let Mr Muckleston know that the just and legitimate renumeration, even of a pauper is not to be shirked by any such discreditable means'.

Had Alfred pushed Edward to his limits and caused him to lose his temper? He was, after all, an intelligent boy and almost certainly not as malleable as his predecessors. Was his temper something Edward had managed to keep behind doors or was it simply a case that, being aware that his employer had a bad reputation, Alfred thought everyone would believe anything he said about him? Knowing Edward's character, we cannot be surprised that this great exploiter of loopholes and well-known miser would take advantage of a system that allowed him to have three months' free labour, nor that he would cast his net far and wide to continue such an advantageous situation. His vast court experience would have allowed him the comfort that, in Alfred's case, there was no written agreement that could be used against him. His letter also re-enforces his well-known poor regard for those whom he sees as of less importance than himself, especially those in his employ. However, never before have we seen any evidence that Edward was a bad-tempered or violent man, something which surely, considering his numerous court appearances, someone else would have mentioned.

The details of the meeting had been reported in the *Alcester Chronicle* alongside a transcript of Edward's letter, with the section where he noted that if the master 'had a nice disposed little boy whom he thought would suit' or a 'nice respectable woman whom he could recommend' or 'did he think that an old man would suit him', raising the comment from the reporter that 'perhaps they would for three months'. It was felt that Edward's assertion that the boy 'must have got into bad company or had bad advice' came with very bad grace from him seeing that the lad had, since he left the workhouse, no other company than that which the reverend gentleman's house afforded. They refrained from commenting on the 'brutality' alleged by the boy, as they could not credit that a minister of religion would be guilty of such conduct.

The day after the board meeting Mr Gothard wrote the following letter to Edward:

Alcester Union Workhouse

May 1st 1890

Dear Sir,

I am instructed by the Guardians of this Union to communicate with you in reference to the boy, Alfred Houghton, from the Union workhouse who you appear to have summarily dismissed from your service, apparently without cause or reason, and without paying him the wages which he was justly and legally entitled to. You must remember than in your correspondence with the Master of the Alcester Union Workhouse in applying to have Alfred Houghton, and also verbally to the Matron when she took him to meet you at Bearley Station, you distinctly engaged the boy on the following terms, viz., to provide him with food and clothing for the first three months, and afterwards to pay him wages at the rate of £6 or £8 per annum. Beyond food, the boy has neither had clothing nor wages, and I am therefore directed to apply to you for the immediate payment of the sum of £4, being eight months' wages at the rate of £6 per annum, due to Alfred Houghton, in respect of and for his services to you, and in default of payment legal proceedings will be forthwith commenced against you to recover the amount. I may say that from enquires the Guardians have made they are quite satisfied that there has been nothing in the boy's conduct to warrant the treatment meted out to him.

I am, Sir, yours obediently,

S. A. Gothard

Clerk to the Alcester Union.

Having waited a week for a response from Edward and having received no reply, he once again wrote:

> Alcester Union Workhouse
> May 9th 1890
>
> Sir,
>
> Not having received any reply to my communication to you in the first instance with reference to the boy, Alfred Houghton, the Guardians will place the matter in the County Court unless they have a satisfactory reply from you on or before Tuesday next.
>
> I am Sir,
> Yours obediently,
> S. A. Gothard

Edward defiantly wrote his reply on a postcard:

> May 12th 1890
> Haseley, Monday
>
> I received your communications. I am prepared to meet your Masters should they deem it necessary to prosecute. I shall give you notice through the proper channels, to produce the agreement, and also two letters written by me to you, dates of which, at proper time I will furnish you with.
>
> Yours,
> Muckleston

When the board met to discuss the situation further, the clerk did agree that there had been no written agreement made with Edward regarding Alfred, but they did have the testimony from the matron who took him to the station. It was also highlighted that the only clothing Edward supplied to Alfred were a few of his own old clothes in which to carry out odd jobs. Although the board was unsure if they had enough evidence for a case, they were all keen to give it a try and agreed to apply to the Alcester Bench or county court for a summons to claim the lost wages.

The people of Alcester, who had undoubtedly been following this case in their local newspaper, had probably hoped to see the spectacle of a real-life minister of religion in the witness box trying to shirk the payment of a poor pauper boy's wages in the local court. They were doomed to disappointment, as the case was set to be heard in the Warwick County Court on 29 June.[235] As soon as he was notified of the summons, Edward paid thirty-two shillings to the court and two shillings for expenses stating that it was 'to be quite sufficient wages having regard to the boys conduct during the time he was in my service'. The guardians had been looking to claim £3-4s-0d and had spent seven shillings bringing the case to court but accepted the payment, which was half of what they were looking for, and withdrew their claim.[236] The minutes of the next board of guardians meeting explained this acceptance, when the clerk reported that the master of the workhouse was by no means satisfied with the behaviour of Alfred Houghton since his return to the union, and the board unanimously agreed that the clerk had acted correctly in agreeing to the lower sum.[237]

The *Alcester Chronicle*, who had previously published almost every word spoken by the guardians relating to the case and had given their own thoughts on the matter, reported the lower payment made by Edward but failed to mention the boy's poor behaviour since he had returned to the workhouse. Although his shaming in the newspapers had been witnessed by many locally, Edward was very fortunate that the national newspapers had not picked up on the story. This situation may have been a wake-up call for Edward as this would prove to be his final dispute with a servant or employee that is known to have reached court. If this situation had been subjected to legal scrutiny it may not have been viewed sympathetically by the bishop, fellow clergy or the wider public.

Alfred went on to better things. At the age of twenty-three he was a baker and had married Clara Bennett in Bidford on 31 December 1900. Initially the couple lived with Clara's parents but soon had a home of their own, but no children, and he remained a baker and confectioner in the village until his death in 1936.

By 5 April 1891, when the census was taken, the family at Haseley were still in the market for a maidservant. At this time the household consisted of Edward, Emily, daughter Mabel and a boy named Arthur Howard, aged fourteen. Arthur had been born in Bristol and was now employed as a general domestic servant. Despite his bad experience with Alfred, Edward had clearly not been deterred from employing boys.

Edward was now in his seventies and rather than spending his time in court, he had found other interests, which would result in a certain amount of fame rather than the infamy of the preceding years.

Chapter Seventeen

Sugar

IN 1898 EDWARD, BEING ALMOST EIGHTY YEARS OLD, received a package of seeds, possibly not realising at the time how important the receipt of this gift would become. Long before 1898 there were concerns being raised about the bankrupt West Indies colonies, the monetary losses being caused by the abolition of slavery and especially the impact of this on the supply of sugar to England. By 1880 Europe had embraced sugar beet and it had become the main source of sugar on the continent but, with Britain having a vested interest in the sugar cane plantations, it was during the First World War, when the usual source of sugar was threatened, that sugar beet was considered a viable crop here. Mr Sigmund Stein, a German sugar expert, had long suspected that it was possible to produce first-class sugar beet in England and, for the purpose of testing his theory, supplied 400 British farmers with the necessary seed free of charge, one of whom was Edward. Most recipients who decided to sow these French and German seeds confined themselves to conducting their experiments on a small scale and, although some fine roots were produced, the area cultivated was too limited for it to be proved whether sugar beet could be grown to advantage in England.

The glebe farmland, a few hundred yards north of the rectory, had been rented out for at least the first fifteen years of Edward's incumbency. The land could be farmed by the vicar or rented out to receive an income, but once the incumbent died or moved on, the land, which belonged to the Church, would pass to his successor. Along with other landowners in the parish, he also had to pay tithes on the land, and as it was a fair-sized farm, it made Edward one of the major landowners in the area.

It is possible that the dispute over the manure with his outgoing tenant, Mr Dorsett, that had seen them meeting in court in 1880, may have put off further tenants. Or was it the refusal of Mrs Brooks to allow him to build a farmhouse on the land that made it difficult to find someone to farm the glebe land? It may simply have been the case that Edward saw the end of the tenancy as an opportunity to take back control of the farm himself and, whatever the reason, by 1881 he was employing a local man, Cornelius Pinfold, as farm bailiff.

By September 1882, Edward was starting to take an increased interest in farming when he displayed what was reported as 'a capital lot of potatoes' at the Horticultural Exhibition in Warwick, although he did not enter them into the competition.[238] The following year he entered a two-year-old dark brown mare, not exceeding 13½ hands, into a best pony jumping competition at Coventry, an event organised by the Warwickshire Agricultural Society, achieving second place.[239] Throughout the following years Edward was recorded as attending various stock sales around Warwickshire, including one where stock belonging to the Marquis of Hertford was sold off at Ragley Park in 1883 and another in 1896 where Kerry and Dexter cattle were being sold by a neighbour. These sales often became social events, and on the latter occasion the Earl of Warwick presided, over a hundred people attended and a luncheon took place in a marquee near the sale ground. Although Edward did not make any purchases on this occasion, a representative of the Prince of Wales clearly thought the cattle of high enough quality to warrant several purchases.[240]

The sender of the seeds, Sigmund Stein, was born in 1861 on a farm in a village called Skopitetz in Bohemia (now part of the Czech Republic). He studied in Vienna for four years and in 1883 graduated in Chemistry, Mechanical Engineering and Agriculture, and went on to specialise in the manufacture of sugar, especially that from sugar beet. After his military service in the Austrian army,[241] he worked in sugar beet factories in Bohemia and Silesia until, in 1890, he was invited by Messrs Crosfield and Barrow to manage their sugar refinery in Liverpool, England. This refinery refined cane sugar imported from the West Indies, but Stein was an advocate for sugar beet and for almost twenty years between 1895 and 1914 he tried to popularise its growth in England. He faced many challenges in his quest, not least from the Cane Sugar Union, who would regularly advertise in the newspapers stating readers should 'beware of spurious European imitations' and that 'beet sugar produces mould in preservations'. Stein became a British subject, married and set up home in Liverpool, residing in a large house in the city at 214 Parliament Street, then a prosperous area.[242]

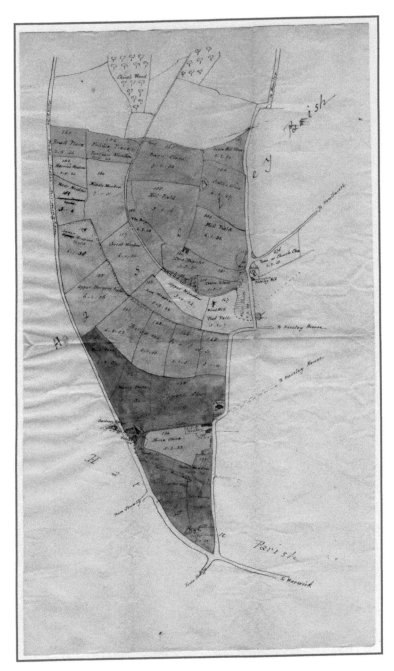

Plan of the glebe land at Haseley.

Edward, never one to turn down something for nothing, made full use of the seeds and had sown a full half acre. When he lifted his first crop on 28 September 1898, he sent samples back to Mr Stein at his base in Liverpool. Referring to Edward's endeavours, it would later be reported that, 'Probably the scheme would have fallen through, at least for the time, had it not been for the energy of the clergyman farmer, who set his lay brethren an example of thoroughness by conducting his experiments on a scale sufficiently extensive to form a really practical test.'[243] Sigmund Stein lectured to farmers all over the country and included details of Edward's successes in his presentations, writing many articles on the subject and even publishing a book entitled *Sugar*.

Such was Edward's fame regarding his sugar-growing activities that in November 1899 his portrait appeared on the front page of the *Sunday Reader Magazine*, accompanied with an article which was full of praise for his endeavours in the growing of sugar beet. It pointed out that agriculture was suffering a depression in England and that the country was becoming reliant on imports, which was a dangerous state of affairs. It explained Edward's successes, pointing out that his sugar beet was a better quality than that being grown in Germany and that other agriculturalists need to 'depart from stereotyped methods and develop all the possibilities of English soil'. Edward was described as 'one of our "fine old English gentlemen" bluff and hearty, who loves a country life, and is deeply versed in matters agricultural, to which he devotes most of the time clerical duties leave him' and that he 'leads a very active life, and by taking such a deep interest in agricultural concerns has formed another tie between himself and his flock, by whom he is much loved and respected'.

Edward had found a new interest and one which came with a certain amount of fame, rather than the infamy of his middle years, and he may have been justifiably proud to read such a glowing testimonial after all the difficulties experienced so far during his incumbency at Haseley. It is not surprising that in February 1899, Edward was elected to the Warwickshire Chamber of Agriculture on the recommendation of his friend and neighbour Sir James Sawyer, who was its chairman.[244] Edward was a regular attendee at the society's meetings during subsequent years.

The quality of the sugar beet crops grown at Haseley continued to be exceptional and Mr Sigmund Stein wrote, 'I may remark and express my best thanks to the Rev. Edward Muckleston, of Haseley Rectory in Warwick, for the help in my endeavours. The Rev. E. Muckleston planted on the Haseley Glebe Farm, in Warwick last year and this year beet roots, which I may say classify amongst the best grown in these islands.' On receiving the annual analysis of his sugar beet, Edward took to sending the report to the local newspapers who were happy to print it. The Shropshire newspapers also picked up on his success and, when printing his reports, pointed out that he was a native of the county and that his ancestors had lived in Shropshire for centuries. At last they were proud to have reason to claim him as one of their own.

A couple of months after the first report on Edward's sugar beet crop appeared in the *Leamington Spa Courier*, the same newspaper published a copy of a certificate of analysis of the sugar beet grown by the Earl of Denbigh. Edward, with more than a touch of egotism, was quick to write to the newspaper, pointing out how much better his sugar beet was and commenting, 'Why mine should be better I am quite puzzled to know, for I took no special pains in manuring, where Lord Denbigh did. I fancy Lord Denbigh over-manured. I used only farmyard manure; my vegetation days were 147 his were 150.'[245]

Edward was now appearing in the newspapers in a very positive light; in February 1900 the *Leamington Spa Courier* reported that, 'Warwickshire is privileged in having professional men like Sir James Sawyer, or politicians like Colonel Victor Milward, who take a deep personal interest in the welfare of a county, which outside of its metropolis, is so exclusively agricultural. Nor are we less

The Rev. E. Mackleston has just received the report of the analysis of his last crop grown in the glebe land at Haseley Rectory. The land on which the roots were grown was sandy with a sandy sub-soil. It was not manured in any way and the previous crop had been peas. The result of the analysis which is very satisfactory is :—

		Compared with F.O. Lieut, Magdeburg, analysed 11th Oct. 1899.
Average weight of roots without leaves in grammes	871	629
Degrees Brix (dry matter)	19·40	18 80
Specific gravity	1·081	1 0780
Quantity of sugar in 100 parts of the juice	16 30	16·08
Quantity of non-sugar in 100 parts of the juice	3 10	2·72
Quotient of purity	84·02	86 63
Quantity of sugar in 100 parts of the roots	15 20	
Shape of roots	well shaped.	

In his concluding remarks the analyst, Sigmund Stein, says :—" These well-shaped roots show a very good result. Weight and saccharine contents are higher than in German grown roots. Quotient of purity is as well satisfactory."

Extract of the newspaper report on Edward's 1899 crop.

fortunate of having clergymen who are keen students of cultivation as well as theology. In the Rev. David W. Sitwell, of Leamington Hastings, and the Rev. Edward Muckleston of Haseley, we have two practical agriculturalists of whom we are not a little proud, and on whose opinions of land questions we value greatly.'[246] Where Edward's farming expertise had come from is unknown, although it could have been down to practical experience or possibly it was the work of his farm bailiff. He now started to experiment and reported on the quality of the sugar beet produced based on the different crops grown in the fields previously, how much manure he had used and how long the crop had been in the ground. Being proud of his success and knowing the great interest taken in all things agricultural by the Countess of Warwick, he forwarded a copy of the report to her ladyship and she replied by telegraph: 'Your letter just received: so sorry am in Scotland, cannot call see roots. Congratulate you warmly on your success in most interesting experiment. Lady Warwick, Stanley, Perth.'

Sigmund Stein was keen to exploit Edward's success, aiming to encourage others to become involved in growing the crop. In 1900 he was to write to Edward, 'Perhaps you would have the kindness to write to the London and Provincial press about the good results you have got in sugar beet growing this year, embodying my analysis and report.'[247] However, the government could not see their way to stopping the bounties on foreign sugar, which meant that it remained cheaper to import the product. When the Warwickshire MP Colonel Milward, a keen advocate of growing sugar beet in Britain, died in 1901, those interested in the crop turned to Mr W. F. Lawrence to be their champion in Parliament. He was the Conservative member for Abercromby in Liverpool, and he had experimented for some years with sugar beet cultivation at Cowesfield in Salisbury. He was a prominent member of the Sugar Committee in the House of Commons and had been in communication with Edward, who was not going to give up the fight and by now had suggested utilising sugar beet for cattle feeding. In writing to Edward, Mr Lawrence commented, 'It seems your results are better than mine, probably owing to less drought from which we suffer. My output is about twelve tons. Cattle will eat beet readily, but our fattening experiments last year gave it no preference over mangolds. The Brussels conference ought to close once and for all the bounty system, when this new industry will benefit our country districts.' Unfortunately for those in the industry, he was mistaken, as the bounties remained in place.

In October 1902, probably due to illness, Edward left it to his bailiff, Cornelius Pinfold, to write to the local newspapers giving an update on the crop results at the farm for that year. In his report he indicated that he was growing wheat, barley, oats, beans, swedes, mangolds and potatoes, as well as sugar beet. Mr Pinfold also pointed out that several farmers in the area had taken up the growing of sugar beet but that the Reverend Muckleston was the most prominent grower.[248] On receipt on the analysis of the 1902 sugar beet samples from Mr Stein, the report was once again sent to the local newspapers. Although still attending occasional meetings of the Agricultural Society, Edward, at eighty-three years old, had handed over much of the cultivation responsibilities to his bailiff and Mr Stein sent him a personal letter congratulating him very heartily on his success, saying, 'The result is really so good that I place your roots in the foremost rank.' It was reported that Mr Pinfold had some of the roots photographed.[249]

The following year Edward announced that the sugar beet grown that year was called White Improved Vilmorin's French, which yielded a very good crop once again.[250] The crop grown in 1904 was to be his last. He had constantly sent his apologies to the Agricultural Chamber meetings during the year, almost certainly due to ill health, and at eighty-five years of age, decided to let the farm and sell off his stock and farming equipment.[251]

Mr Webber of the nearby Firs Farm had also decided to retire and advertised in the same newspaper, although Edward had the advantage, as his auction was scheduled to take place the day before his neighbour's sale.

GLEBE FARM, HASELEY,
Three and half miles from Warwick and one mile from Hatton Station.

HUTTON, THOMPSON, AND COLBOURNE

Are favoured with instructions from the Rev. E. Muckleston (who has let the Farm), TO SELL BY AUCTION, on MONDAY, SEPTEMBER 26th, 1904.

21 HEAD of CATTLE. 8 SHEEP, 4 Pigs, 2 Work Horses, the whole of the capital Agricultural Implements, Gears 2 Ricks of Clover, Rick of Oats, 13 Geese, 30 Couples of Fowls, and about half an Acre of growing Potatoes.

Sale at Twelve o'clock. Catalogues on application.

Stock and equipment sale in September 1904.

The new tenant of the farm continued to grow sugar beet until 1907, and Edward duly arranged for the roots to be tested and the analysis sent to the Warwickshire and Shropshire newspapers. Mr Stein was to say that the 1905 sugar beet from the Haseley Glebe Farm had the best result of any he had received all year, and Edward was said to be rather proud of this fact.[252] He continued to be an advocate for the growing of sugar beet in England, reporting that Mr Stein was intending to open a factory for sugar beet in the Midlands during 1905, and if he did, 'it will be the greatest benefit the English farmer has ever experienced'.[253] Another newspaper article the same year was to report, 'someday the dream of such enthusiasts as Mr Muckleston, will be realised, and the manufacture of sugar will become a profitable industry in this country'. Unfortunately, sugar beet could only be grown in certain localities, and for a successful sugar refinery there needed to be at least 10,000 acres of the crop within easy reach of the factory.[254]

In 1906 it was reported that growing sugar beet was being trialled at five different locations in Essex. The previous year Lord Denbigh had approached the government with a view to securing facilities that would encourage English farmers to grow the root, but then there was a change of parliament.[255] Lord Denbigh did indeed pick up the question in the House of Lords, where he mentioned Edward's long and significant experiments with the crop.[256] He pointed out that it was a new industry that could not sustain the excise duty of 4s-2d [approximately £16 today] per hundred weight but might reasonably be able to pay 2s-6d [approximately £10 today]. Although this proposal had some support within the House on the basis that, once the industry matured, they could increase the duty, there were some objections and the proposal for reducing the duty was not passed.[257]

By 1907 Edward, at the age of eighty-eight, was no longer attending meetings of the Agricultural Society and this would also be the last year that he sent in his sugar beet certificate. His experiments had not been forgotten and at meetings, such as the one held in 1910 of the Ludlow Agricultural Society addressed by Professor Sigmund Stein, Edward's experiments at Haseley were still being referred to. The argument from the Ludlow farmers was that other crops were more profitable, but Mr Stein produced facts and figures to show that growing sugar beet was viable and profitable, and as a result the Earl of Plymouth and Lord Inchiquin, who both farmed near Ludlow, expressed interest in carrying out experiments in growing the crop on their farms.[258]

It was the mid-1920s before sugar beet was grown on a large scale in the United Kingdom, mainly in response to the sugar shortages seen during the First World War and, as such, seventeen autonomous processing factories were built after the war. Today sixty per cent of the United Kingdom's sugar comes from sugar beet, processed by British Sugar.[259]

A few seeds had given Edward a new purpose in his later years and he was deservedly very proud of his achievements, which were important agriculturally at the time and endeared him to the local community. He died before the outbreak of the war, but he may have been looking down from heaven, noting the sugar shortages and saying, 'I told you so, you should have listened to me.'

Chapter Eighteen

A Special Friendship

I F THE *SUNDAY READER* PUBLICATION OF 1899 IS TO be believed, Edward, who was now eighty years old, had changed from being litigious, belligerent, selfish and disliked by his parishioners, to someone who was 'bluff and hearty and much loved and respected by his flock', although clearly his ego had not dissipated. What could possibly have brought around this change; was it simply that he was growing older or was he, as I suspect, being influenced by a new friendship? His financial situation, although never to be as it once was, had also improved.

Sir James Sawyer was a prominent physician working at Queen's Hospital, Birmingham and in a secondary role as the consulting physician for Birmingham Children's Hospital.[260] He was knighted by Queen Victoria in 1885, had purchased Haseley Hall from Sir Edward Antrobus in 1889 and lived there for the rest of his life. The twenty-four-roomed residence was a mile and a half north of the rectory and its inhabitants were parishioners of Edward's, with St Mary's being Sir James's local church. Not only would Edward and Sir James, who was twenty-five years younger, become great friends who would socialise together, but Edward would also appoint him as vicar's churchwarden every year until his death. The parish had two churchwardens: one whom was elected by and represented the people of the parish, whilst the second was chosen by and spoke for the vicar. The other local-landed gentleman, Alfred Hewlett, of forty-seven-roomed Haseley Manor, and ten years Edward's junior, was elected annually as the people's churchwarden. Prior to Sir James moving to Haseley, there had been some tension between Edward and Alfred Hewlett, but on Sir James's appointment the three gentlemen began to work well together on parish business, which removed an element of conflict from Edward's life. The annual vestry meetings were often reported upon and the accounts were always found to be satisfactory; any minor shortfall in funds was subsidised by Alfred, who was the Lord of the Manor.

Sir James was a staunch Conservative and whether this had always been Edward's persuasion or if he was influenced by his friend is not clear, but Edward attended meetings and speeches being given by the local Members of Parliament, such as the one held by Mr Chaplin at Warwick in March 1889.[261] Also reported in the local newspapers was his attendance at the meetings of the Warwickshire Chamber of Agriculture to which he had been elected in 1899 by Sir James who was chairman of the society.

A day of perfect weather in the summer of 1893[262] saw Edward and daughter Mabel, as well as Mr and Mrs Hewlett, visit Haseley Hall, where a picnic was being held as part of an excursion of the ladies of the Working Men's Conservative Club and the Ladywood Habitation of the Primrose League. Sir James and Lady Sawyer were president and ruling councillor of the two bodies respectively, and they and their children were hosting the event which would subsequently be held annually. There were around 200 people in attendance, who enjoyed themselves by exploring the surrounding woods and fields, gathering flowers and blossoms, playing cricket, and participating in other amusements. Whilst the substantial picnic was being enjoyed on the lawn, the Old Reservoir Band played. Afterwards the whole of Sir James's home was freely thrown open to the visitors, who derived great pleasure from its inspection.[263]

An incident that took place in the autumn of 1891 would seem to indicate that there was still some ill will between certain factions within the parish. There was a small dispute when the gamekeeper of Haseley Manor claimed to have seen Edward's bailiff, Cornelius Pinfold, shoot a pheasant without having a game licence. When this case came to court, a labourer by the name of John Mason testified that Cornelius was helping him to thatch a rick on behalf of Edward and did not leave his side for more than five minutes. The court believed that the distance between the two spots where the men were supposed to be standing was too far to be sure of what had taken place and dismissed the case.[264]

Financially things improved slightly for Edward and his family when, in 1892, his wife's uncle, Reverend Henry Cautley Holmes, the Vicar of Garthorpe near Melton Mowbray, took his own life by throwing himself down a well. The inquest gave a verdict of suicide whilst temporarily insane, and it appears that the seventy-eight-year-old was unnecessarily worried about money and his health.[265] In his will dated earlier that year he left Emily, his niece, an annuity worth £16 a year for life [about £1,300 today]; and to her son Charles Edward Muckleston, then aged seventeen, he left £200 [about £16,500 today] to be given to him on his eighteenth birthday. Charles also received Henry's watch and chain, his manuscript sermons, and mathematical manuscripts.[266]

At the Easter vestry meeting held in March 1894 Edward proposed the purchase of a beautiful sacramental paten from the period of William and Mary, to be used in the church in conjunction with the well-known ancient silver chalice belonging to the parish. It was decided to set up a subscription list, which was supported by all those present.[267] The silver chalice remains in the church to this day.

On 23 September that same year, a harvest festival was held at St Mary's, with Edward conducting the service and the Reverend G. E. A. Pargitter MA, of St Paul's in Leamington, was invited to deliver a sermon. The decoration of the church was impressive and almost every resident contributed either corn, fruit or flowers. Mrs Hewlett sent a profusion of palms, other pot plants, cut flowers and various fruits, most notable amongst which were peaches and some remarkably fine bunches of grapes. Lady Sawyer also sent some beautiful grapes and flowers. The decoration was carried out by Miss Hewlett, and Edward's wife and daughter. There was a very full congregation and as a result the offertory amounted to £2-14s-6d [about £220 today] and this sum was used to pay off the debt incurred in purchasing the paten proposed at the earlier vestry meeting. The fruit and flowers were sent to the Warneford Hospital.[268] Harvest festivals became an annual event at the church during the remainder of Edward's time at Haseley and on most occasions the offertory was sent to the same hospital along with the fruit and flowers. It appears to signal a wider acceptance of Edward as the parish priest.

Several meetings were held to decide whether Haseley should have a parish council or simply hold a regular parish meeting to discuss local issues. The decisive meeting took place in February 1895 at a time when Edward was indisposed and unable to attend, and so we are unaware of his thoughts on the matter. Alfred Hewlett was the chairman and clearly in favour of a parish meeting, although others were in favour of a council, including Cornelius Pinfold, Edward's bailiff, and on a vote, it was decided in favour of a parish council. Mr Hewlett stated that although he was not in favour of a council himself, he hoped they could work harmoniously together. He would forward the resolution to the proper quarter, inform the parishioners of any reply and then call a further meeting.[269] Haseley did obtain a parish council; five councillors were elected annually and Edward at one time took on the role of chairman of the council.[270]

Now that Sir James was living at Haseley Hall, an active social life ensued, including annual garden parties and other events that Edward and his family were invited to. Emily often assisted Lady Sawyer in organising the village fetes. One such event was the coming-of-age celebrations held by Sir James and Lady Sawyer in honour of their eldest son. This took place at their home over a weekend in September 1895 and was attended by the Muckleston family. After tea Edward stepped forward and addressed Sir James and Lady Sawyer, saying that he was speaking on behalf of all those present in offering sincere congratulations on the coming of age of their eldest son. They wished him every possible happiness and prosperity and would like him to accept a pair of silver backed brushes that his well-wishers in the parish had purchased. He went on to say that Sir James and his family were held in high esteem and respect by everyone in the neighbourhood. This speech was followed by a round of applause, and everyone, having previously been supplied with wine, drank to the health of the young squire.[271]

Possibly inspired by their neighbours, and at the invitation of Edward and Emily, the married women of the parish assembled at the vicarage to inaugurate a branch of the Mothers' Union in Haseley.[272] A nice tea was provided and Emily said a few words to open the meeting that was also attended by Lady Sawyer, although Mrs Hewlett was too ill to attend.[273]

The death of Edward's cousin, Reverend Rowland Muckleston, on 8 April 1897 heralded what was to be an eventful year. He had been Dean of the Oxford College when Edward was taking his degree and later became vicar of the rural parish of Dinedor in Herefordshire. He also assisted as an examiner at Oxford University and made his name by translating books, such as the Scandinavian legend of Frithiof, into English. He had amassed quite a fortune; his will being valued at £68,435-6s-1d [over £5 million today], the majority of this being left to various charities. Although not mentioned in his original will, Rowland had added a codicil in 1888 leaving Edward the sum of £1,000 [about £78,000 today]. For someone who had spent almost a decade living on an annual income of just £80, this was a massive financial improvement for Edward. In a later codicil Rowland also left Edward the portrait of his grandmother, Mrs Mary Muckleston née

Fletcher, who was also Edward's great-grandmother, and in a further codicil he left £2,000 [about £155,000 today] to Edward's son Charles.

This was also the year when Queen Victoria's Diamond Jubilee was the centre of many celebrations, including the annual garden party at Haseley Hall, but this year the event was also to honour Sir James's eldest daughter Maud's coming of age. There were about a hundred guests at this event, who were, for the most part, from the parish of Haseley, a few from Shrewley and a few of the Sawyers' friends from Birmingham. After tea, the male portion of the villagers received a pipe and tobacco from Mr Edward Sawyer, and they proved themselves accustomed and vigorous smokers. The health of Sir James and Lady Sawyer was proposed by Edward and this toast was drunk to musical accompaniments, the company having been liberally supplied with wine.[274]

Having had a window commissioned in the church of St Chad in Shrewsbury on the death of his father and now having some money, Edward decided that he would also have a window fitted in the chancel at Haseley to commemorate

Memorial window in the chancel of St Mary's church, Haseley.

both his mother and Queen Victoria. His mother had died six years earlier at the age of eighty-seven; her estate, valued at less than £100 [about £8,000 today], went to her unmarried daughter, Mary Louisa, with whom she had been living. In September 1897 an elegant and artistic stained-glass memorial window was fitted in the chancel of St Mary's Church, the subject being the Visitation of the Virgin Mary to Elizabeth, her cousin who was pregnant with John the Baptist, as recorded in the Gospel of Saint Luke. Above the two figures was a scroll containing the words 'Blessed art thou among women'. Underneath was the following inscription surmounted by a crown: 'Erected to the Glory of God by Rev Edward Muckleston in memory of his mother, Elizabeth Muckleston and to celebrate Queen Victoria's Diamond Jubilee 1897.'[275]

If anything was to show how the Mucklestons had now conformed to expectations, then it was evidenced in September 1897, when many of the women and children of the parish of Haseley were entertained to tea at the rectory. In addition to the rector and his family, those present included Lady Sawyer and the Misses Sawyer, and Mrs and Miss Hewlett. The tea was followed by a sale of work, most

Inscription of the memorial window in St Mary's Church, Haseley.

of the articles having been made by the working party in connection with the Mother's Union. The proceeds were devoted to the church expenses. During this occasion Emily was presented with a handsome chased silver bowl, gold-lined and subscribed for by the parishioners, in recognition of her valuable service in voluntarily training the choir for twenty-five years. Mrs Hewlett spoke of the respect and esteem in which the vicar's wife was held and Emily, in a few words, expressed her gratitude for the handsome present and her appreciation for the kind feeling which had prompted the gift.[276]

Having lived modestly with her family at Ford Hall, later that year Edward's widowed sister, Elizabeth Lyon,[277] also passed away, her husband and Edward's official patron having died in 1880. Her personal estate was worth just £1,862-13s-11d [about £145,000 today] and was left to her son, Frederick Corbett Lyon. Sometime after 1903, several years after their mother's death, her two surviving and unmarried children, Frederick and Mary Julia, then both in their fifties, were to leave Ford and settle in Cheltenham. The reason for this move, and so far away from the only home they had known, is unclear, as Frederick was financially comfortable, employing a cook, a housemaid and a coachman at their new fourteen-roomed home. It is possible that the lease of Ford Hall came up for renewal and the owner decided not to renew it, or maybe, as they were ageing, the fact that Cheltenham was a spa town may have been the attraction. For Mary Julia especially, it was a wrench to leave the village.

Perhaps inspired by the inheritance of his great-grandmother's portrait and his improved financial situation, Edward decided to commission one of his own. The artist that he decided to sit for was the Irish painter John Nunn Bolton, who was mainly known as a landscape painter, but on moving to Warwick had also started painting portraits and miniatures, gaining quite a reputation for himself. Aged just twenty-eight at the time, he was employed by Edward. He passed away in 1909 at the young age of thirty-nine, having exhibited at the Royal Hibernian Academy, Royal Society of Artists Birmingham, Leeds and Manchester Art Galleries, and at the Royal Academy. The record price for one of his paintings is £8,433; this was a landscape sold by Sotheby's in the USA. Edward chose to be painted in oils and wearing his university robes, which depicted the fact that he held a MA degree.

Edward's children were growing up and immersing themselves in parish life. Aged twenty-seven, Mabel had an accident and fell off her bicycle near Kenilworth railway station at around two o'clock and became unconscious.[278] When recovered, she found that her purse had been stolen from her pocket.[279] Mabel could also be found advertising puppies for sale, although there is no evidence to show that this was a commercial enterprise.[280]

During breaks from university, Edward's son Charles also became involved in local events, especially those of a sporting nature; becoming a member of the committee organising the athletics contest at the tenth annual flower show for Rowington, Hatton and district, which took place in a field on Sir James Sawyer's property.[281] Both Charles and Mabel regularly sang in local concerts, usually to raise funds for various charitable purposes and sometimes accompanied by their mother on the piano.

In the 1890s an annual outing for the Haseley church choir and bell ringers was instigated, mainly funded by the Hewletts, with a few other parishioners contributing. Edward, and sometimes Emily, joined the group, visiting such seaside towns as Aberystwyth in Wales[282] and Weston-super-Mare in Somerset.[283]

As a sign of his acceptance by the wider community, when Princess Christian, born Princess Helena the fifth child of Queen Victoria, came to Leamington to open a new wing on the Warneford Hospital in January 1900, Edward was invited to the ceremony.[284]

At the start of the new century, the senior church officials were starting to look at some of the livings. In the Worcester diocese alone there were sixty parishes having a population of under 300, Haseley had 208, and it was agreed that if a married man was appointed to a parish, that the living needed to be worth at least £400 a year [over £30,000 today].[285] Many of the smaller parishes brought in far less than this and the church was starting to look at their viability; it was agreed that, as soon as one of them became vacant, Haseley would be merged with the parish of Hatton.

After a long reign which saw many changes throughout the empire, Queen Victoria died in 1901, and on the day of her burial a memorial service was held at Haseley.[286] The altar, pulpit, reading desk and the lectern were draped in purple cloth. Over the reredos was hung a large and handsome red ensign. The litany and burial service were used, and suitable hymns were sang, one, called 'God Rest Our Queen', being specially composed for the occasion. Edward, who was just six days younger than the deceased monarch, officiated. At the close he gave a feeling and appropriate address, in which he alluded to the fine character of the late lamented Queen and gave expression of the love and admiration felt for her by all, and to the worldwide regret at her loss.[287]

The first census of the twentieth century shows that the Muckleston household consisted of eighty-one-year-old Edward, Emily, Mabel and once again a young servant named Ellen Moore, aged fourteen, who had been born in Hereford.

On the coronation of King Edward, a dinner and tea took place by the kind invitation of Mr Hewlett of Haseley Manor held in a large marquee near the Beausale school, with the residents of the wider locality of Beausale and Honiley also invited.[288] It commenced at 2pm when all the men and women sat down to a substantial dinner. At 4pm the women and children sat down to a good tea and afterwards the residents of Haseley presented Mr Hewlett with a handsome silver cigar holder in a Russian leather case, and to Mrs Hewlett a large lady's work basket. The gifts were presented in the name of the parish by Mr Webber of the Firs Farm, who spoke of the very good feeling which existed towards Mr and Mrs Hewlett during their long residence in the neighbourhood and of their numerous kindnesses extended to all. These remarks were seconded by Edward, who heartily agreed with all that Mr Webber had said. Both Mr and Mrs Hewlett responded, giving thanks for the warm words and gifts.[289]

In 1902 Edward knew that he was now fully accepted in local society when he was invited, alongside other nobility and churchmen in the area, to act as a vice president for the Warwick and Leamington Lifeboat Saturday Fund[290] and less than a month later he attended Lady Warwick's garden party held at Warwick Castle over the first weekend in August. At the gathering he met with Indian royalty and many colonial guests, including governors and senior-ranking army officers.[291] In October Edward and his two children attended a reception at the town hall in Leamington, following the unveiling of a memorial to Queen Victoria.[292]

At the annual vestry meeting held in 1903,[293] Lady Sawyer, Mrs Hewlett and Mrs Muckleston, who were clearly regarded as the leading ladies of the parish, were given a hearty vote of thanks for their invaluable help in raising the money necessary for restoring the fabric of the church. The church accounts had an adverse balance of almost £5 [about £400 today], but as usual Mr Hewlett covered the shortfall.[294]

Sir James Sawyer appears to have had a very positive influence on Edward's life and behaviour, and was able to engender a lot of goodwill in the parish with the church at its centre. Having grown up as a member of the gentry, Edward probably felt that he should be socialising with people of Sir James's and the Earl and Lady Warwick's standing, and altered his behaviour such that he was seen in a positive light by his peers. He was, however, getting older, and the last decade of his life would have many highs and lows.

Chapter Nineteen

Demise

THE NEW CENTURY SAW SEVERAL FAMILY celebrations. Edward's son Charles had achieved his Bachelor of Arts degree from Cambridge University in 1900, having entered in 1894, and, like his father, taking a significant amount of time to earn his degree; it would not be until 1913 that he obtained his master's degree. Charles followed in his father's footsteps, taking the Church as his vocation, and he was ordained at St Thomas' Church in Chester on 7 June 1903 by the Bishop of Chester, Francis Jayne, who then appointed Charles to assist as a curate at Sandbach in Cheshire.[295] This was followed on 14 July by his marriage to Louisa Gwendoline Morgan, the daughter of the late Canon Morgan of Glenogwen where the ceremony took place.[296]

The wedding was especially pretty. Louisa had tastefully chosen a gown of embroidered chiffon over white satin, caught up with sprays of orange blossom and myrtle, and trimmed with rich lace. On her head she wore a tulle veil over a wreath of natural orange blossom, fastened with a pearl brooch her mother had given her as a wedding present.

Around her neck sparkled a magnificent pearl heart-shaped pendant centred with diamonds and emeralds, a gift from the bridegroom. He had also spared no expense on the bridesmaids; his gift to the adult bridesmaids were four-leaved shamrock opal scarf pins and the two little girls received gold-enamelled pendants.

The church, decorated with white flowers and hothouse plants, was packed with guests while curious onlookers crowded around the entrance. I imagine they marvelled at the spectacle of the bridal pair and their entourage. A delicate contrast met the eye between the four adult bridesmaids in pale blue, crepe-de-chine over silk, with yokes of straw-coloured lace and the young girls in their white Liberty silk frocks. The dresses of the older bridesmaids, who included Charles's sister Mabel, were set off by blue and biscuit straw hats, wreathed with tiny white roses and tied with black velvet. Colour was added by the bride's mother dressed in black and white voile, and the bridegroom's mother in a pink purple shade known as heliotrope. Louisa's older brother, Dunlap Morgan, who gave her away, and the best man, Reverend Edgar Hollins, completed the wedding party. The reception was held at the home of the bride's mother at Maes-y-Groes. The newly married couple left for a honeymoon in Paris and the Swiss Lakes.

Presents to the bridal pair featured items of furniture from the immediate family. Edward gave an antique inlaid cabinet; Emily a Chesterfield coach and two easy chairs; Charles's aunt, Mary Louisa, gave a French hall clock; and his sister Mabel gave a tantalus cabinet for keeping spirits under lock and key, safe from children and servants. Many of Charles's wealthy new parishioners at Sandbach gave individual presents, others contributed to a collection for a silver tea and coffee service. The parishioners of his former home parish of Haseley presented a handsomely bound bible with the inscription, 'Presented to the Rev. C. E. Muckleston, B.A. on the occasion of his marriage, 14 July 1903, by a few of the residents in his native parish of Haseley, with their best wishes for his future welfare.' The long list of presents itemised in newspaper reports round off with various silver items, notably a case of six silver apostle spoons which were popular at the time, a Worcester tea service, cut glassware and even some opera glasses for the groom.[297] A Mr J. S. Hughes of Repton, Derbyshire, who two years later would become part of the family, was also in attendance.

As the present list indicated, Victorian homes were very cluttered, as can be seen in the photograph of Edward

A photograph of the drawing room at Haseley Rectory.

and Emily's drawing room at Haseley Rectory taken a few years before his son's marriage.

One can only imagine Edward's joy when, on 23 October 1904 at Park House in Sandbach, Cheshire,[298] what would turn out to be his one and only grandson was born and named John Corbett Muckleston. The name Corbett being the maiden name of the baby's eight times great-grandmother, an heiress who had brought a significant amount of land and money into the family. The family line would now continue for a further generation but, although John would marry, he would not have any children, and as such would be the last of Edward's descendants.

Meanwhile Mabel and Emily were continuing their good work in Haseley and would often be found singing locally to raise funds, such as at the concert in aid of the Haseley and Hatton Working Men's Club held in January 1904.[299] This year Mabel also stood for election to the Warwick Rural Council, having been proposed by Cornelius Pinfold, her father's bailiff; her opponent was William Gibbs, a local farmer.[300] The 1869 Municipal Franchise Act gave the vote to some women ratepayers in local elections and also enabled women to serve as Poor Law Guardians. The 1888 County Council Act also gave women the vote at county and borough council elections.[301] However, even though women could stand for rural councils like this since 1894, it was not until 1907 that they could stand in city, borough and county elections. There were some underhand tactics to try and prevent Mabel from standing so that Gibbs was unopposed, but Pinfold was made aware of the shenanigans and ensured that her application was received by the relevant parties in good time.[302]

On 30 March the election took place at the Beausale schoolroom, with both candidates taking great interest in the proceedings. The voting was rather slack during the afternoon but was better in the evening, with the final count being seventeen votes for Mabel and eleven for William Gibbs.[303] She attended the first meeting of the newly formed Warwick Rural District Council held at the workhouse on the afternoon of Saturday 16 April, and was appointed to the House Committee.[304] She was also appointed to the Warwick Board of Guardians and carried out the responsibilities required of both positions with enthusiasm. She received a letter congratulating her on her success from Mr John Hughes and they had clearly kept in touch since her brother's wedding.[305]

As a further sign that he was now held in high regard, Edward was asked to assist at the important wedding of the Honourable Thomas Lemuel James, journalist, banker and former Postmaster General of the United States, who took Edith Louisa, the only daughter of Mr and Mrs William Gardner Colbourne of Stratford-upon-Avon, as his third wife. The wedding took place at Holy Trinity Church in the bride's hometown.[306]

Edward was now eighty-four years old, and his health was starting to fail, causing him to send a letter of apology for his absence at the 1903 Easter Vestry meeting held at the Falcon Inn. He received a letter back from those attending the meeting with their sympathies for his indisposition. His health improved sufficiently to allow him to attend the Thanksgiving service for the harvest in October, although he restricted himself to just reading the prayers, most of the service being taken by the Reverend H. Temple Robson, the Rector of Honiley, who preached an excellent sermon assisted by Sir James Sawyer, who read the lesson. As usual the church was beautifully decorated by Emily and Mabel, ably assisted by Miss Hewlett and Miss Sawyer. The contributions of corn, fruit, flowers and vegetables were abundant.[307] Acting as curate, Samuel Joseph Walker MA had assisted with the parish duties[308] whilst Edward had been indisposed, but Edward was well enough to conduct the wedding at Haseley church between Amy Sawyer, the daughter of his good friend Sir James, and Dr Herbert Finch, a fellow physician.[309]

Edward's health improved during 1905 and that year he was able to attend the Easter Vestry meeting[310] and some of the Chamber of Agriculture meetings. In May he had the honour of assisting at a second Sawyer marriage, when the elder daughter of Sir James married Mr Harry Stallard, but with the Reverend J. T. Evans of Stow in the Wold conducting most of the service.[311] Many of Edward's official church duties were now being carried out by other clergymen, mainly from the adjoining parishes.

On 25 May 1905 Edward's daughter, Mabel, married widower Mr John Spittle Hughes of Repton, Derbyshire in surprising circumstances. You might have expected the wedding to be in Haseley; instead it took place at St George's Church, Hanover Square, London, the same church where her parents had married, and one considered a fashionable place for society weddings. The ceremony was performed by Mabel's brother, Charles, and her cousin, Reverend F. Trafford Morgan Payler, and she was given away by her mother. It was reported that the ceremony was 'confined to members of the contracting families'.[312]

It is not clear whether Edward had attended the ceremony, and he was certainly not mentioned in any newspaper reports. The reason may have been that he was not well enough to give his daughter away, or perhaps it was that he disapproved of the marriage, explaining why it did not take place at Haseley. Mabel was thirty-two years old and her new husband, a hop merchant previously trading in iron, coal and coke, was sixty-five years old, this being a slightly larger age gap than that of her parents' when they married. John Hughes also had a daughter by his first marriage who was ten years older than his new bride. Although Mabel had not married locally, the parishioners of Haseley presented her with a beautiful standing work basket in pale blue and white wicker, handsomely lined with pale blue quilted satin and fitted with mother of pearl implements of all kinds required for needlework. She was to say amongst the many beautiful presents received that she would 'always treasure this one in remembrance of those amongst whom she passed many happy years.'[313] The local council also congratulated her on her marriage at the meeting held in June.[314]

Both children now married and living some distance away, the household now comprised Edward, Emily and a servant. Edward had periods of indisposition, but there were still quite a few occasions when he attended the Chamber of Agriculture and Conservative Association meetings, the garden parties held at Haseley Hall, and participated in key events at the church, including the annual outings with the choir. Most of the baptisms and marriages during this period were conducted by other local clergymen, as they were planned events and arrangements could be made. Edward did, however, conduct several burials. When he first arrived in Haseley there was a large drop in church attendance but, as an example of how his parishioners had changed their opinion of the rector, the Harvest Festival service taken by Edward in 1906 was attended by over 240 people, with many having to stand outside due to the compact size of the church.[315] As the population of the parish at this time was only 208, the event had clearly attracted people from far afield.

In 1907, his wife Emily followed in their daughter's footsteps by becoming the representative for Haseley on the Rural Council and board of guardians, the same year son Charles was appointed Vicar of Sandbach Heath in Cheshire, a position he would hold for the rest of his life.

A period of ill health for Edward coincided with a visit to Haseley made by the Bishop of Worcester, Huyshe Yeatman-Biggs, on Tuesday 31 March 1908. He was the

Sandbach Heath Church.

fourth bishop that Edward had served under since coming to Haseley. In the absence of the rector his Lordship was received by the Reverend Dr Dickins, Rural Dean and Rector of Emscote; the Reverend J. C. Patterson Morgan of the Hartlebury College of Clergy; the Reverend R. J. Hopkins, Vicar of Hatton; the Reverend R. A. Lamphugh, who was acting as a curate at Haseley, and Mr J. S. Hughes, Mabel's husband. The bishop delivered a very impressive address that was much appreciated by the congregation, which included representatives of every family in the parish. He wanted to 'try and raise their thoughts upwards, from the small interests of earth, to those that would bring them a happy immortality when they had passed through the gates of death unto eternal life'. After the service, there was a large gathering for tea at the rectory, after which the bishop visited Edward in his sickroom.[316]

Six months later Edward was well enough to join the choir on their annual outing, this time to the Imperial International Exhibition at White City in London. It was a long day travelling by train, as they started out at 8am in the morning, returning at 3.30am the next day.[317] A month later, eighty-nine-year-old Edward attended the Thanksgiving service at the church but was not well enough to participate.

In April 1909, Edward and his children, along with their spouses, attended the funeral of his youngest sister, Mary Louisa, who had died aged eighty-six at her home, Maple Lodge, in Shrewsbury. Her niece and nephew, Mary Julia and Frederick Lyon, also attended the private funeral at St Chad's in Shrewsbury. After an impressive service, she was interred in the family vault and the local newspaper was to say, 'her death was keenly felt by rich and poor, with whom she was universally a favourite'.[318]

The following year, a week after he attended a memorial service for King Edward VII at St Mary's, Edward received the news that his daughter's husband, Mr John Hughes, had passed away. He was seventy-one years old and had been ill for several months. The funeral, which was conducted by Mabel's brother Charles, took place on 2 June 1910 in Repton, Derbyshire. There were two notable absences from the funeral, as neither Edward nor Mr Hughes's daughter by his first marriage attended the ceremony.[319] Mabel was a widow after just five years of marriage.

Mabel and her brother, Charles, were named as executors of her husband's will, and as a sign of the estrangement between his daughter and his new wife, John Hughes had made it very clear as who had what in his will by writing, 'in order to prevent any dispute between my said daughter Constance Mary Owen Hughes and my said wife'. John Hughes had use of properties and lands, which had been inherited through his wife, and he wished his daughter to be offered these properties as part of her inheritance; everything else was to be sold, and in essence both wife and daughter inherited half of his estate which was worth £2,089 [approximately £165,000 today].

When the annual Thanksgiving service took place later that year, Edward had just recovered from a serious illness, which had also kept Emily from her council and board of guardian meetings, as she needed to care for him. He was well enough to give the blessing, although the Vicar of Honiley conducted the rest of the service, assisted by Sir James Sawyer.[320]

By the time that the 1911 census was taken, widowed Mabel had returned home to Haseley and, along with Edward and Emily, a twenty-two-year-old servant called Rose Shilton made up the household. Although made fragile by age, in general this was to be a better year health-wise for Edward, now in his nineties, and he was well enough to assist in the marriage of Sir James Sawyer's son, which took place at St Mary's church. This would be the last wedding that Edward would be involved in as, although he would attend some of the vestry meetings, most of the work relating to the church would fall to his churchwardens and neighbouring vicars: Edward just attended the occasional ceremony at key times of the year to give the blessing. Mabel was now at home and able to take care of her father, when needed, allowing Emily to resume her council and board of guardian duties.

On 8 July 1912, Edward's nephew, Frederick Corbett Lyon, the son of his sister Elizabeth, died at the age of sixty-five. At the time of his death he was living at 14 Pittville Lawn, Cheltenham, with his only surviving sister, Mary Julia. Frederick's estate was valued at £8,585-17s-5d [approximately £650,000 today], and Mary Julia was both executrix of his will and sole beneficiary.[321] None of Elizabeth's children ever married.

The last ceremony Edward was to attend at the church was the Harvest Thanksgiving held on 5 October 1913, when he was described as the venerable Reverend Muckleston.[322] He then suffered a bout of bronchitis, which was to last twenty-five days leading to his death on Wednesday 26 November 1913 at the age of ninety-four.

Edward's obituary appeared in several newspapers in both Warwickshire and Shropshire. His illustrious ancestry

191 5		Registration District WARWICK.						
		DEATHS in the Sub-District of WARWICK in the County of WARWICK.						
Columns :— 1.		2.	3.	4	5.	6.	7.	8.	9.
No.	When and Where Died	Name and Surname	Sex	Age	Rank or Profession	Cause of Death	Signature, Description, and Residence of Informant	When Registered	Signature of Registrar
81	Twenty-sixth November 1913 The Rectory Haseley	Edward Muckleston	Male	74 years	Clerk in Holy Orders	Bronchitis 25 days certified by Herbert Tibbits M.B.	Emily Muckleston Widow of deceased Present at the death The Rectory Haseley	Twenty-eighth November 1913	P. Loy Registrar

Edward's death certificate.

was mentioned, as was the fact that although he was unable to walk much in his later years, prior to his indisposition he had thought nothing of walking twenty miles a day.[323] All the obituaries were completely complimentary and there was no mention of his various antics when younger.

It was cold but dry as the funeral took place at St Mary's, Haseley on the afternoon of Monday 1 December. The organist, Mr Lawrence Mason, played the death march as the cortege came into the crowded church, the coffin being borne by six of his former parishioners, Mr Dodd of the Glebe Farm, Mr Taylor of Cheney's Farm, Mr Gibbs of Haseley Green Farm, Mr George Hancox, Mr Ludlow and Mr Barker. It was followed by the principle mourners being his surviving family, which consisted of his wife, son and daughter, daughter-in-law, and his niece. The service was conducted by three fellow clergymen: the Reverend H. Temple Robson Vicar of Eastern Green, the Reverend R. J. Hopkins Vicar of Hatton and the Reverend A. W. Horton of Leamington, and many other clergymen were in attendance. The church was crowded with sorrowing parishioners, gentry and other friends from a wide area around Haseley who had come to pay their last respects to their venerable rector who had lived amongst them for forty-eight years. Sir James and his family, and Mrs Lant, the new owner of Haseley Manor, could also be seen amongst the congregation. The coffin was of polished oak with brass mountings and bore the inscription, 'Edward Muckleston, died November 26th, 1913 aged 94'.

The service was partly choral; two hymns were sung by the choir – 'On the Resurrection Morning' and 'A Few More Years Will Roll' – and as the coffin was carried from the church the organist played 'O Rest the Lord'. The grave, on the left of the path leading from the rectory to the church, had been beautifully lined with moss and white flowers by Mr Warren, the head gardener at Haseley Manor. There was an abundance of floral tributes, consisting of no less than thirteen wreaths, six crosses, two sprays and two chaplets. One of the crosses carried the message, 'In loving memory of a dear friend dating from Shrewsbury days. May he rest in peace.'[324]

Inscription on Edward's grave reads, 'Edward Muckleston Rector of Haseley 48 years died November 26 1913 aged 94 years and Emily Muckleston his wife died December 23 1937 aged 92 years'.

Edward's grave (photograph taken in 2019).

During Edward's ninety-four years on earth he had experienced many highs and lows: he had been rich, even carrying the title Lord of the Manor, but he had also been poor, being reduced to living on the equivalent of a curate's wage for almost a decade; he had been both despised and loved, infamous and famous, cruel and kind, and maybe his God had granted him a lengthy existence to allow him the chance to redeem himself before his death, an opportunity that Edward clearly embraced.

Epilogue

E DWARD'S PASSING RESULTED IN THE PARISHES OF
Haseley and Hatton merging into one, with the then-
Rector of Hatton, the Reverend R. J. Hopkins, taking on
the additional duties of the united parishes. What the
Brooks family thought of this decision, and how they were
impacted following decades of court cases unsuccessfully
trying to wrestle back the right to appoint the Vicar of
Haseley, is not known. Emily and Mabel now had to look
for a new home, and three months after Edward's death
they left the parish where they had lived for most of their
lives. Before she left Emily was presented with a very pretty
Russian handbag[325] and a purse containing ten guineas
[over £800 in today's terms] by the parishioners of Haseley
as a token of their esteem.[326] The two widows settled in
Leamington Spa just over seven miles away, finding a home
at 38 Heath Terrace, where they continued to be part of the
community, assisting at fetes and other charitable events.

Back in Haseley, on 30 January 1919, just over five
years after Edward's death, his friend and neighbour, Sir
James Sawyer, died at Haseley Hall and was buried at St

Mary's Church, where he had been Edward's long-standing churchwarden. Sir James had retired in 1891 but had kept his medical links by delivering the Lumleian Lecture to the Royal College of Physicians in 1908, the subject being maladies of the heart. He had also been president of the Birmingham Conservative Association and Warwickshire Chamber of Agriculture, two organisations in which he had been heavily involved. His death occurred only a few months after that of Frederick Hewlett, the people's churchwarden, who had served under Edward for many years. As such, it truly marked the end of Edward's links to Haseley.

Sir James Sawyer's grave at St Mary's Church, Haseley.

In contrast to his father, Edward's son, Charles, spent the rest of his days as Vicar of Sandbach Heath, leading a conventional life and behaving as one would expect a rural vicar to behave. When war broke out, he was thirty-nine years old and by the time conscription came into force he was too old to fight. Vicars were exempt from conscription due to their own vital role in the community, although many did volunteer to go with the troops. Charles carried out the duties of a rural vicar in wartime, raising money through concerts, events and collections. In July 1916 his twelve-year-old son John also participated in raising funds and collected 10s 7d towards the effort to help the Serbians. Both Charles and Louisa, his wife, were theatrical and good singers, and were active participants in social events in and around Sandbach. Throughout the war Charles carried out workhouse duties at Arclid and regularly chaired meetings at the National School. In 1917 when a Voluntary Aid Detachment (VAD) hospital, which aimed to take care of wounded soldiers, was planned at Abbey Fields in Sandbach, Charles was appointed secretary.[327] He was struggling financially and, as one of the main beneficiaries named in his cousin, Mary Julia Lyon's, will, he found it necessary to approach his cousin for financial support and she gave him an advance of £1,150, adding a codicil to her will saying this amount was to be deducted from what he would have received on her death. In January 1929, almost certainly to improve his income, he placed an advertisement in the *Yorkshire Post* offering board and tuition with 'delicate and backward boys especially considered'. The education was to take place at his large vicarage, which had 'grounds and all modern conveniences'.[328]

The grave of Charles Edward Muckleston in front of the church at Sandbach Heath. His wife and his son are also buried in the same grave.

Just over three years later, on 19 April 1932, at the relatively young age of fifty-six, Charles passed away, leaving Louisa a young widow.[329] He had a heart condition and in his last days also suffered from pneumonia, and he may have been too ill to put his affairs in order. Charles had made his will in August 1903, a month after he married and before his son was born, and when he was probably in a much better position financially; this had never been updated. When his will was proven, it was recorded that he had no real estate, the vicarage belonging to the Church, and his net worth was just £118-18s-11d [around £5,500 today]. Charles had named two executors with a payment of £50 to each for their trouble, £100 to his sister, Mabel, and the rest of his estate to be invested in a trust fund and the income to his wife for her life. After his wife's death, the entire trust fund was to go to Charles's sister. Under the circumstances I think it is unlikely that the executors and Mabel were interested in taking what was offered in his will.[330] Repeating history, Louisa now had to leave the vicarage and find a new home, as her mother-in-law had done before her.

Charles had been well respected and the parishioners of Sandbach Heath, where he had been vicar for twenty-five years, raised funds to purchase gifts for the church in his name. The Archdeacon of Macclesfield dedicated them in front of a large congregation and all three gifts were suitably inscribed. They consisted of a handsome oak credence table, a pair of massive brass candlesticks for the altar and, for the font, a mother of pearl shell mounted in silver with a silver Maltese cross for the handle.[331]

John Corbett Muckleston, twenty-seven years old at the time of his father's death and who had chosen not to follow his father's and grandfather's vocation, was a salesman and probably in a position to support his mother. Four years after his father's death, John married Dorothy Astley at Acocks Green in Birmingham.[332] The bride looked charming in ivory satin and orange blossom, with a Honiton lace veil lent by an aunt; she carried a lovely bouquet of lilies, the gift of the bridegroom, and her father gave her away.[333] The couple honeymooned in Wales and then went to live at The Bungalow in Honiley, less than three miles from Haseley where his father had grown up; it was also less than ten miles from his grandmother and aunt's home in Leamington. John may have known the area from holidays spent at his grandparents as a young child. Dorothy would hold whist drives at her home and was, for a couple of years, organist at Great and Little Packington Churches. She resigned this position in August 1938 to take up similar duties near home, and it is possible she played at St Mary's in Haseley.

By 1940 the couple were breeding puppies, including fox terriers, wire terriers and Dalmatians, and offering them for sale. They also sold chickens, including Island Red Cockerels, Rhode Island Reds and laying hens. In 1941 they sold a large quantity of household furniture, and it was possibly at this time that they moved away from the area. By 1949 the couple were living in Church Stretton near Shrewsbury in Shropshire. John was aged thirty-five to forty during the war years and as such would have been eligible for conscription, but he did not fight. Those in the farming industry were exempt from being called up, and his chicken-farming business may have put him in this category. It is also possible that he had a health issue which prevented him participating in the war.

John's ageing grandmother Emily did not live to see the outbreak of war. Like her husband, Edward, Emily lived a long life, passing away at her home at 38 Heath Terrace, Leamington Spa on Thursday 23 December 1937, aged ninety-three. Her obituary mentioned that she was for many years a member of the Warwickshire Board of Guardians, that her daughter had succeeded her in that capacity, and it also mentioned her long service as organist at Haseley Church. Emily's funeral took place five days later at Haseley, where she was interred in the same grave as her husband. Her remaining family – daughter Mabel, grandson John and his wife, and daughter-in-law Louisa – all attended her funeral. Among the wreaths were ones from Mary Julia Lyon, her husband's niece and members of the Sawyer family.[334] In her will Emily left the trust fund, which had been set up for her in 1868, to her daughter, and her estate was recorded as worth just under £5,000 [about £250,000 today].

Edward's last surviving niece, Mary Julia Lyon, was also long lived, dying in a nursing home on 31 January 1940 at the age of ninety-one. She was the youngest and the last survivor of the Lyon siblings. Her obituary was entitled 'A Life of Quiet Service'. She still owned the house at 14 Pittville Lawn in Cheltenham, where she had lived for almost thirty years, having moved there from Ford with her brother. Her ancestry through her father's line was the same as that of the then-Queen, Elizabeth Bowes Lyon, making them distant cousins. Her parents had moved to Ford from the Lyon family seat at Llanyblodwell Hall, Montgomeryshire; her mother, being a Muckleston, could trace her ancestry back to the thirteenth century.

Mary Julia took no part in the public activities of the town of Cheltenham, instead choosing to support various causes and charities which appealed to her heart and faith in an unassuming way with constant cheerfulness. Until the last she never failed to attend Trinity Church twice on every Sunday, even though she was both blind and deaf. Supported by her maids, she attended public prayers in all weathers, although she could hardly hear a word. She was buried at Ford, the village she loved.[335] Her estate was originally recorded as having a value of £13,379-4s-8d [around £525,000 today] but was later re-sworn by her executor, the solicitor Charles Alan Reynolds, to be just £2,887-16s-11d [about £115,000 today]. It was not unusual for estate values to be re-sworn; the first figure was often an estimate and the re-sworn figure would be the final statement of its true value when probate was completed. Mary Julia had outlived most of her Lyon and Muckleston cousins and had attached numerous codicils to her will, in which she left £200 to augment the living of Trinity Church and £100 to the Society for the Assistance of Ladies in Reduced Circumstances. There were also bequests to servants and friends, and £200 to her cousin's son, John Corbett Muckleston. She left her house to Geraldine Daniels, who was probably a friend or companion, as she was no relation. She left all her silver plate bearing the Lyon coat of arms to a distant Lyon relative and that bearing the Muckleston coat of arms to her cousin Mabel. She requested that the rest of her estate be shared between Mabel, who was to have half plus £1,150, and the other half, less the £1,150 previously gifted to her cousin Charles, was to be shared between his widow, Louisa Muckleston, and her son, John Corbett Muckleston. When all the bequests were paid, there was not much left for Louisa and John.

Having parents who both lived into their nineties, Mabel could have reasonably expected to live to a great age, but her life was cut short by a tragic accident. Mabel was seventy-seven years old and living at Southedge, Lillington Avenue, Leamington Spa, when on Monday 31 October 1949 her neighbour, Frederick Harvey, was delivering a letter to her house and noticed that her milk and bread were still on her doorstep; knowing that the baker had not been since Saturday, he entered Mabel's house and found her dead in a gas-filled room. At the inquest, her nephew John testified that his aunt had no worries and a police officer, PC Evans, said he had conducted an experiment and found that on boiling a kettle on a gas ring in the room, just a few drops of water spilling over put out the flames. The county pathologist, Dr Prior, said that the cause of death was carbon monoxide poisoning and that it was possible to go to sleep and absorb the gas without knowing it. The coroner gave a verdict of death by misadventure and ruled out suicide.[336] Mabel's funeral took place at Lillington Parish Church on 8 November and she was buried in the churchyard.[337] Mabel had inherited money from her husband, mother and cousin Mary Julia, and was a wealthy woman; she did not leave a will but, being the only surviving blood relative, her nephew John Muckleston applied to administer, and no doubt inherited her estate, which was valued at £29,585-14s-10d [just under £1 million today].

Mabel's sister-in-law, Louisa Gwendoline Muckleston, who was most commonly known as Gwendoline, passed away on 20 July 1954, aged seventy-seven, at the Belvedere Hotel in Church Stretton, Shropshire. For many years prior to her death she suffered several illnesses and her daughter-in-law Dorothy had cared for her. She was buried alongside her husband at Sandbach Heath; her estate was valued at £486-0s-8d [about £11,500 today], inherited by her son, John Corbett Muckleston.[338]

John Corbett Muckleston was now Edward's only surviving descendant and, on moving from Warwickshire, he and his wife Dorothy Amy had settled at Church Stretton, where his mother was living, possibly with a view to caring for her. By 1952 the couple had moved to live in the imposing Lawley House at Leebotwood, close to

Lawley House, Leebotwood.

Church Stretton, just south of Shrewsbury. He had, by this time, decided to concentrate on poultry farming; it was in this year that the National Domestic Poultry Keepers Council was set up and John was elected to the Executive Committee at its first annual conference.[339] He had become a well-known lecturer at domestic poultry keeper's clubs in the Midlands and spoke on the Conservative Farming Policy at conservative clubs in 1953.[340] John had also been chairman of the Shropshire branch of the National Farmers Union (NFU) and was very upset when, at their show in 1959, they served synthetic cream and no eggs in their tent.[341] In 1960 he was elected to the Egg Marketing Board as member for the West Midlands, achieving a majority of almost 9,000 votes over the sitting member, a Mr Ernest Pattison of Stone in Staffordshire.[342] Clearly popular in the role and with elections being held every three years, he held this position until 1969, obtaining very large majorities, choosing at this point to step down.

Evidencing that he had inherited at least a little bit of his grandfather's eccentricity, John was to make local government history in 1967. He had been asked to stand for the All Stretton Parish Council, as it seemed unlikely there would be enough candidates to fill all three vacancies; he agreed simply to keep the seat warm until someone else was found and he was duly nominated. As it happened, there were five candidates in the end and an election had to be held. John tried to withdraw but was told it was too late, as his name had been entered on the ballot papers. He duly went out to canvass but asked everyone in the parish not to vote for him; he was a busy man and did not want the position and did not even vote for himself. The result was that he did not receive a single vote, the first time this had ever happened in local government history, a situation so bizarre that it was even

John Corbett Muckleston (with the walking stick).

reported as far afield as the United States. John took it as a vote of confidence, as it showed that his campaign had worked, and the electors had taken him seriously when he had asked them not to vote for him.[343]

By 1968, now sixty-four years of age, and possibly with one eye on retirement, John arranged for valuable portraits and miniatures, ornamental items and furniture dating from the seventeenth to nineteenth centuries to be sold at auction in Leamington Spa. These included two silver pepper shakers dated 1749 and 1772, and a military dressing case which probably belonged to his great-grandfather. These were undoubtably family heirlooms, including portraits of his ancestors, but John was the last of the line descended from 'Captain' Muckleston and he had no children to leave them to.[344] He had been involved with the poultry trade for almost forty years, but his retirement was short as, just five years later, on 19 June 1974 at the age of sixty-nine, he passed away at his home, The Courtyard, Cound Hall, near Shrewsbury.[345] His estate was valued at £14,238 [about £110,000 today], which he left to his widow.[346]

John's widow, Dorothy Amy Muckleston, survived him by more than seventeen years, dying on the 10 October 1991, aged eighty-three. She left many bequests to charities, including Age Concern, Doctor Barnados, The National Trust and local organisations, such as Cound Parish for the maintenance of the church. After a few bequests to friends, she left the remainder of her estate to her brother, Kenneth Loade Astley, his wife and her niece, Hazel Astley.[347] The Muckleston family pedigree, created by her husband's great-aunt, Mary Louisa Muckleston, was left to Shropshire Archives where it remains today.

Images from the Muckleston pedigree created by Mary Louisa.

Index

Timeline of Key Events in Edward's Life

Date	Event
6 June 1819	Edward is born.
7 July 1819	Edward is baptised.
17 September 1820	Edward's sister Elizabeth is born.
9 May 1825	Edward's sister Mary Louisa is born.
Circa 1825	Edward and his family move to live at Bicton House.
1832–1838	Edward attends Shrewsbury School.
1835	Edward's family leave Bicton House and move to Quarry Place.
28 February 1839	Edward enters Worcester College at Oxford University.
1840	Edward is made a burgess of Shrewsbury.
25 April 1845	Edward achieves his BA degree.
14 June 1845	Edward's father borrows £1,000 from Charles Darwin towards his daughter Elizabeth's marriage settlement.
26 June 1845	Edward's sister Elizabeth marries William Lyon.
Early 1846	Edward is ordained a deacon.
1846–1848	Edward is curate of Welsh Hampton.
1846	Edward attends his first Shropshire Hunt Ball.
21 December 1846	Edward is ordained a priest.

19 June 1847	Edward achieves his MA degree.
2 February 1848	Edward's father arranges for him to receive the rents from some properties.
24 November 1849	Edward becomes curate at Mackworth in Derbyshire.
Early 1850	Edward is licensed to the curacies of Chaddesden and Stanley in Derbyshire.
May 1851	Edward resigns his curacies in Derbyshire.
21 June 1851	Edward's father dies.
Late 1851	Edward becomes perpetual curate of Ford.
26 December 1851	Charles Darwin asks his accountant to chase Edward, as his father's executor, for the money owed on a mortgage which was overdue.
Early 1853	Edward had the window dedicated to his father erected in St Chad's Church.
20 December 1853	Edward is given six months to pay the money owed to Darwin.
11 July 1854	Edward makes payment of the money and interest owed to Darwin.
24 November 1855	Edward makes his first known court appearance when he brings a tenant to court.
25 March 1856	Edward purchases Ford Hall in Ford Shropshire.
1856–1857	Edward is curate at King's Heath in Worcestershire.
January 1859	Muckleston v Trentham is heard in court at Shrewsbury.
6 February 1860	Edward is observed acting suspiciously around his neighbour's trees.
2 April 1860	Edward is in front of the petty sessions relating to the damage to the trees.
4 April 1860	Edward is once again seen acting suspiciously around his neighbour's trees.
16 April 1860	A meeting of the ratepayers of Ford took place to discuss their vicar's behaviour.
27 April 1860	Edward is once again in court relating to the damage caused to his neighbour's trees.

29 & 30 April 1860	A meeting of all parishioners takes place at Ford to discuss their vicar's behaviour.
4 June 1860	Edward conducts his final baptism at Ford.
18 July 1860	The Bishop of Hereford accepts Edward's resignation from his position of Vicar of Ford.
1860	Edward rents out his house at Ford to his brother-in-law.
7 April 1861	On the census Edward records himself as a clergyman without cure of souls.
Circa 1861/2	William Lyon purchases the right to appoint the next Vicar of Haseley in Warwickshire.
1861–1862	Edward is curate of Warsop in Nottinghamshire.
7 May 1862	Edward takes the GWR to court following an uncomfortable journey.
June 1862	Edward exhibits a specimen of hard building stone from one of his quarries at the International Exhibition.
22 March 1863	Tittensor v Muckleston is heard at Shrewsbury County Court.
October 1863	Rees v Muckleston heard by the magistrates.
March 1865	Edward buys himself of a charge of fare-dodging.
10 June 1865	William Lyon appoints Edward Rector of Haseley.
September 1865	Edward takes up his appointment at Haseley.
December 1866	Muckleston v the London and North West Railway Company heard in Bloomsbury in London.
26 September 1867	Edward is taken to court by the GWR for fraudulent journeys made on their trains.
October 1867	Edward avoids a further court summons by the GWR by paying a large sum into their staff benevolent fund.
1868	Edward arranges for the Chancel at St Mary's at Haseley Church to be extended.
February 1868	Edward's sister Mary Louisa puts a complaint before the Court of Chancery relating to money owed to her by Edward.
12 Feb 1868	Edward takes out a mortgage for £2,400 on his estates at Worthen.

15 March 1868	Edward sells a lead mine he owns to Mr Charles Rule.
December 1868	Edward purchases a lead mine at Pontblyddyn in partnership with a Mr Peake.
June 1869	Edward and his partner borrow £900 from the Chester Benefit Building Society to enable them to purchase a mine.
July 1869	Edward and Peake dissolve their partnership in a lead mine due to Peake's bankruptcy.
October 1869	Clarke v Muckleston in Chancery.
19 November 1869	The Chester Benefit Building Society bring a charge of larceny against Edward and his foreman, a Mr Guest.
4 December 1869	The Sheriff of Warwickshire asked to serve a writ on Edward regarding Mary Louisa's successful claim in Chancery.
7 December 1869	Edward appears on a list of bankrupts in the *Shipping and Mercantile Gazette*.
Early 1870	The Chester Benefit Building Society take ownership of the mine and sell it to redeem the mortgage.
11 March 1870	Meeting at the Birmingham Bankruptcy Court to discuss Edward's bankruptcy.
6 April 1870	Edward attends the bankruptcy court to answer questions regarding his financial affairs.
May 1870	Edward's lands and Lordships are advertised for sale as part of his bankruptcy.
27 September 1870	Edward's bankruptcy is reported as discharged.
1870–1878	A sequestrator was appointed to manage the Haseley benefice.
26 April 1871	A further meeting of Edward's creditors is held at the bankruptcy court asking for a suspension of the discharge of bankruptcy.
10 May 1871	A further bankruptcy hearing is held as further assets had come to light which had not previously been declared.
June 1871	A large quantity of rare old ports, choice sherry, etc., which belonged to Edward were advertised for sale.
27 July 1871	Edward marries Emily Holmes.

12 June 1872	Edward and Emily have a daughter who they call Mabel Emily.
28 June 1873	Edward's mother dies.
23 March 1875	Gubbins (his washerwoman) v Muckleston is heard at Warwick.
5 June 1875	Edward is again taken to court by the GWR for failing to pay his fare.
7 October 1875	Edward and Emily have a son who they call Charles Edward.
29 March 1876	Edward's housekeeper at Haseley, Mary Blower, dies.
13 Feb 1877	Blower v Muckleston is in court.
1878–1888	Edward conflicts with the corporation regarding the Mill Pool.
1879	Charles Rule and accomplices are charged with using the mine he had purchased from Edward fraudulently.
3 March 1879	Edward's tries to obtain permission to build a farmhouse on the Glebe Farm.
8 March 1880	Edward's brother-in-law William Lyon dies.
January 1881	Muckleston v Rawlings is heard in court at Warwick.
January 1881	Muckleston v Dorsett is heard on the same day.
1881	Edwards v Muckleston is heard in court at Warwick.
1882	Edward displays potatoes at the Horticultural Exhibition.
1883–1890	Edward is providing a testimonial for tooth block in the newspapers.
1885–1887	Conflict over the site of the new burial ground at Haseley.
29 June 1889	Edward agrees to take a boy called Alfred Houghton, from the Alcester Board of Guardians, to act as his page.
1890	Edward becomes a Director of George Gunn (Limited) Cereal Food Manufactures.
24 April 1890	Edward complains to the board of guardians about Alfred Houghton.
27 April 1890	Alfred Houghton writes to his mother complaining as to how he is being treated by Edward.

1 May 1890	The clerk to the Alcester Union writes to Edward requesting Alfred Houghton's wages.
May 1890	The Alcester Board of Guardians agree to take Edward to court of the matter of the outstanding wages.
July 1890	Edward settles his dispute with the Alcester Board of Guardians.
1891	Sir James Sawyer takes up residence at Haseley Hall.
8 October 1891	Edward is taken to court by a firm of solicitors.
23 September 1892	Emily's uncle Henry Cautley Holmes dies.
1894–1900	Edward's son is studying for his BA at Cambridge.
8 April 1897	Edward's cousin Rowland Muckleston dies.
September 1897	Edward installs a memorial window at Haseley Church.
1897	Edward has his portrait painted by John Nunn Bolton.
11 November 1897	Edward's sister Elizabeth dies.
1898	Edward received a packet of sugar beet seeds from Sigmund Stein.
February 1899	Edward is elected to the Warwickshire Chamber of Agriculture.
1900–1904	Edward is actively growing and promoting sugar beet.
1902	Edward becomes a vice president for the Warwick and Leamington Lifeboat Fund.
1903	Edward is starting to have periods of ill health.
14 July 1903	Edward's son Charles Edward marries Louisa Gwendoline Morgan.
January 1904	Edward's daughter Mabel is elected to Warwickshire Rural Council and Board of Guardians.
September 1904	Edward gives up farming.
23 October 1904	Edward's one and only grandson is born and is named John Corbett Muckleston.
25 May 1905	Edward's daughter Mabel Emily marries John Spittle Hughes.
1907	Edward is no longer attending Chamber of Agriculture meetings.

1907	Edward's wife Emily is elected to Warwickshire Rural Council and Board of Guardians.
1907	Edward's son Charles is appointed Vicar of Sandbach Heath in Cheshire.
25 March 1909	Edward's sister Mary Louisa dies.
July 1909	Brooks v Muckleston relating to the advowson.
June 1910	Edward's son-in-law John Spittle Hughes dies.
8 July 1912	Edward's nephew Frederick Lyon dies.
26 November 1913	Edward dies.
1 December 1913	Edward is buried at Haseley.
19 April 1932	Edward's son Charles Edward dies.
5 August 1936	Edward's grandson John marries Dorothy Astley.
23 December 1937	Edward's wife Emily dies.
31 January 1940	Edward's niece Julia Lyon dies.
31 October 1949	Edward's daughter Mabel Emily dies.
19 June 1974	Edward's grandson John Corbett, the last of his descendants, dies.

Bibliography

Aldcock, Professor Derek H. and Freeman, Michael J. (1986) *Transport in the Industrial Revolution*, Manchester University Press.

Barrett, Andrew and Harrison, Christopher (1999) *Crime and Punishment in England*, UCL Press Limited.

Cowrie, L.W. (1996) *The Wordsworth Dictionary of British Social History*, Wordsworth Editions Ltd., Hertfordshire, England.

Davis, J. (1984) *A Poor Man's System of Justice: The London Police Courts in the Second Half of the Nineteenth Century*. The Historical Journal, 27(2), 309–335. doi:10.1017/S0018246X00017817

Ellis, Roger (1997) *Who's Who in Victorian Britain*, Shepheard Walwyn (publishers) Ltd.

Foster, Joseph (2000) *Alumni Oxoniensis 1500–1886* (Fascimile Edition), Thoemmes Continuum.

Fowler, Simon (2014) *The Workhouse: The People, The Places, The Life Behind Doors*, Pen and Sword Books Ltd.

Harris, Donald F. (2012) *Muckleston v Darwin*, Shropshire Family History Society Magazine Article.

Hawkings, David T. (1992) *Criminal Ancestors*, The History Press.

Heald, Henrietta (1992) *Chronicle of Britain and Ireland*, J L International Publishing.

Lewis, Samuel (1848) *A Topographical Dictionary of England*, S. Lewis London.

Woodward, Sir Llewellyn (1962) *The Oxford History of England, The Age of Reform 1815–1870* (2nd Edition), Oxford University Press.

Image Credits

(page numbers to be updated once ready to print)

Page

51   International Exhibition at Kensington. Source: https://en.wikipedia.org/wiki/1862_International_Exhibition. Public domain image.

58   Copy of the advertisement relating to the sale of the presentation rights. Source: *Leamington Spa Courier*, 4 April 1857. Reproduced with kind permission of the British Newspaper Archives.

66   The Rectory at Haseley in the early 1900s. Reproduced with kind permission of Warwickshire County Record Office PTR 82/2019-20. Document reference PH352/88/11/1202.

67   St Mary's Church at Haseley. Author's own photograph, 2018.

69   Interior of St Mary's Church, Haseley. Author's own photograph, 2018.

92   Estate Map of Edward Muckleston's lands. Reproduced with kind permission of Shropshire Archives. Document reference D3651-B-165-31.

96   Advertisement from *Birmingham Daily Post*, 6 July 1871. Reproduced with kind permission of the British Newspaper Archives.

99   Advertisement from *Eddowes Journal*, 1 April 1874. Reproduced with kind permission of the British Newspaper Archives.

107   Advertisement for Tooth Block, *Warwick and Warwickshire Advertiser*, 29 March 1884. Reproduced with kind permission of the British Newspaper Archives.

107   Tomlinson & Hayward advertisement, *Morning Post*, 18 July 1890. Reproduced with kind permission of the British Newspaper Archives.

122   Mary Ann Blower's grave marker. Author's own photograph, 2019.

128   Advertisements relating to servants placed in Warwick and Warwickshire Advertiser, 29 August 1885 and 15 May 1886. Reproduced with kind permission of the British Newspaper Archives.

139   Haseley Water Mill after its closure (circa 1950s). Reproduced with kind permission of Warwickshire County Record Office PTR 82/2019-20. Document reference MWA2625.

160   Plan of the Glebe Land at Haseley. Reproduced with kind permission of Warwickshire County Record Office PTR 82/2019-20. Document reference CR3134/46.

163   Newspaper report from *Warwick and Warwickshire Advertiser*, 28 October 1899. Reproduced with kind permission of the British Newspaper Archives.

166   Newspaper advertisement of stock and equipment sale at the Glebe Farm. Reproduced with kind permission of the British Newspaper Archives.

175   Memorial window, St Mary's Church, Haseley. Author's own photograph, 2018.

176   Inscription on the memorial photograph. Author's own photograph, 2018.

184   Photograph of the drawing room at Haseley Rectory in 1899. Reproduced with kind permission of Warwickshire County Record Office PTR 82/2019-20. Document reference PH1035/C7667.

189   Sandbach Heath Church. Author's own photograph, 2018.

193   Edward's death certificate. Obtained by author from the GRO.

195   Edward Muckleston's grave. Author's own photograph, 2019.

197   Sir James Sawyer's grave at Haseley churchyard. Author's own photograph, 2019.

199   Charles Edward Muckleston's grave. Author's own photograph, 2019.

205   Lawley House Leebotwood. Source: photograph submitted to TripAdvisor by Helene R (November 2011).

206   John Corbett Muckleston (with the walking stick). Reproduced with the kind permission of Shropshire Archives. Document reference 5843/7.

208   Images from the Muckleston Pedigree. Reproduced with the kind permission of Shropshire Archives. Document reference 5843/1.

Endnotes

Chapter One

1   Dates given on a family pedigree drawn up by Mary Louisa Muckleston and deposited in Shropshire Archives, reference 5843/1.

2   On 7 July 1819. St Mary's Shrewsbury Parish Registers, source Shropshire Archives.

3   On 17 September 1820.

4   On 9 May 1825. Dates given on a family pedigree drawn up by Mary Louisa Muckleston and deposited in Shropshire Archives, reference 5843/1.

5   1835 Sales Particulars for Bicton House available at Shropshire Archives, reference 4843/2, and Edward Muckleston Account books 1817–1834, Warwickshire Record Office, reference DR0118/20/21.

6   http://www.nationalarchives.gov.uk/currency-converter

7   Edward Muckleston Account books 1817–1834, Warwickshire Record Office, reference DR0118/20/21.

8   Edward Muckleston Account books 1817–1834, Warwickshire Record Office, reference DR0118/20/21.

9   Shrewsbury School Register 1798–1908.

10   https://www.shrewsbury.org.uk/features/school-history, accessed November 2018.

11   https://originalshrewsbury.co.uk/visit/quarry-park, accessed November 2018.

12   Copy of a letter deposited by John Corbett Muckleston with the family pedigree, reference 5843/1.

13   *Alumni Oxonienses 1500–1886.*

14   *Alumni Oxonienses 1500–1886.*

15   *Oxford University and City Herald*, 26 April 1845.

16   On Thursday 10 June 1847, source *Eddowes Journal*, 23 June 1847.

17   On 24 June 1844.

18   On 26 December 1845.

19   Article in the *Shropshire Family History Magazine* December 2012 by Donald F Harris.

20   Shrewsbury Burgess Rolls, sourced at Shropshire Archives.

Chapter Two

21 *London Morning Post*, 29 December 1846.
22 *Derbyshire Courier*, 2 January 1847.
23 Welsh Hampton Parish Registers, sourced at Shropshire Archives.
24 Welsh Hampton Parish registers, sourced at Shropshire Archives.
25 https://www.english-heritage.org.uk/learn/story-of-england/victorian/religion/
26 1851 Gazetteer.
27 *Eddowes Journal*, 1 December 1847.
28 Ford Parish registers.
29 On 2 February 1848.
30 Draft Security Edward Muckleston Snr., to Rev. Edward Muckleston, Shropshire Archives, reference D3651/D/44/211.
31 Samuel Lewis's *A Topographical Dictionary of England, 1848.*
32 John Marius Wilson's Imperial Gazetteer of England and Wales, 1870–1872.
33 *Inverness Courier*, 1 November 1849.
34 *Oxford Chronicle*, 23 March 1850.
35 *Derby Mercury*, 8 January 1851.
36 *Derbyshire Courier*, 22 February 1851.
37 *London Evening Standard*, 27 February 1851.
38 He died in September 1853, source *Limerick Chronicle*, 17 September 1853.
39 In Chaddesden from March 1850 to April 1851 and in Stanley April 1850 to April 1851.
40 *Derby Mercury*, 21 May 1851.

Chapter Three

41 *London Morning Chronicle*, 30 June 1851.
42 From death certificate of Edward Muckleston senior.
43 *Shrewsbury Chronicle*, 13 June 1851.
44 Index to Death Duty Registers 1796–1903, source Findmypast.
45 On Thursday 26 June, source St Chad's Burial Registers, Shropshire Archives.
46 British Army Officers' Widow's Pension Forms 1755–1908, sourced at Findmypast.
47 Article in the *Shropshire Family History Magazine* December 2012 by Donald F Harris.
48 Mortgage Document, reference X3432/13 at Shropshire Archives.
49 Letter dated 26 December 1851 – letters sourced from the Darwin Project https://www.darwinproject.ac.uk/, accessed November 2018.
50 On 20 December 1853.
51 https://www.darwinproject.ac.uk/ contains letters relating to this situation.
52 *Shrewsbury Chronicle*, 4 February 1853,

Chapter Four

53 *Shrewsbury Chronicle*, 23 January 1852.
54 *An Architectural Account of the Churches of Shropshire*, Part 6, pages 526–7.
55 St Michael's Church, Ford, Shropshire, Facebook page https://en-gb.facebook.com/stmichaelsford/about/, *accessed November 2018.*
56 1856 Post Office Directory for Shropshire.

57   *Salisbury and Winchester Journal*, 27 December 1851, page 4 column 6.

58   Ford Parish Registers, sourced at Shropshire Archives.

59   In June 1852.

60   *The Globe*, London, 7 June 1852, page 4 column 3.

61   *Eddowes Journal*, 20 July 1853, page 2 column 3.

62   https://www.archerygb.org/about-us-structure-safeguard/about-us/history/

63   *Eddowes Journal*, 8 August 1855, page 6 column 4.

64   *Shrewsbury Chronicle*, 20 July 1855, page 8 column 1.

65   *Hereford Journal*, 8 August 1855, page 3 column 5.

66   Various editions of the *Shrewsbury Chronicle* listed game licences that had been granted.

67   *Punch Magazine*, 16 October 1875.

68   The attendance information has been obtained from various editions of the *Shrewsbury Chronicle*.

69   *Eddowes Shrewsbury Journal*, 16 January 1856, page 5 column 2.

70   *Hereford Journal*, 2 November 1853, page 2 column 3.

71   https://www.rct.uk/about/press-office/press-releases/queen-victoria-and-the-crimea#/

72   On Saturday 24 November.

73   *North Wales Chronicle*, 1 December 1855, page 7 column 5.

74   In January 1859.

75   *Shrewsbury Chronicle*, 21 January 1859, page 6 column 3.

76   *Shrewsbury Chronicle*, 25 February, page 7 column 4.

77   http://www.kingsheathhistory.co.uk/history1.htm

78   *Aris's Birmingham Gazette, 02 May 1859.*

79   *Worcester Herald*, 19 September 1857, page 4 column 3.

Chapter Five

80   Shropshire Archives bankruptcy paperwork, reference MI5546/2/1.

81   On Tuesday 25 March 1856.

82   On Friday 6 August 1858.

83   On Friday 3 September 1858.

84   *Shrewsbury Chronicle*, 3 September 1858, page 1 column 4.

85   On Monday 2 March 1863.

86   *Shrewsbury Chronicle*, 6 March 1863.

87   Ford Parish Records, reference P110/F/3/1 at Shropshire Archives.

88   In January 1859.

89   *Shrewsbury Chronicle*, 21 January 1859, page 6 column 3.

90   Between 1839 and 1849.

91   *Shrewsbury Chronicle*, 4 April 1860, page 2 column 2.

92   On Wednesday 4 April 1860.

93   Eddowes Shrewsbury Journal 2 May 1860 page 6 column 3

94   On Friday 27 April.

95   *Eddowes Shrewsbury Journal*, 2 May 1860, page 6 column 3.

96   *Shrewsbury Chronicle*, 4 May 1860, page 8 column 4.

97   *Shrewsbury Chronicle*, 11 May 1860, page 3 column 4.

98 On Monday 16 April 1860.

99 On Tuesday 29 May 1860.

100 Diocesan papers concerning Reverend Edward Muckleston in Hereford Archives, reference HD 10/16/15.

101 *Aris's Birmingham Gazette*, 28 July 1860.

Chapter Six

102 In May 1860.

103 *Eddowes Journal*, 16 May 1860.

104 On 5 March 1862.

105 She had to leave on Lady Day 1863.

106 http://www.nationalarchives.gov.uk/education/resources/currency-converter-1270-2017/

107 *Eddowes Journal and General Advertiser for Shropshire and the Principality of Wales*, 14 October 1863.

108 *North Wales Chronicle*, 5 October 1861.

109 *North Wales Chronicle*, 16 November 1861.

110 *Cheltenham Looker On*, 21 December 1861.

111 In December 1861.

112 *Reading Gazette*, 10 May 1862.

113 In June 1862.

114 https://archive.org/details/fournationalexhi00lowe/page/n10

115 *Shrewsbury Chronicle*, 23 May 1862.

116 *Shrewsbury Chronicle*, 13 June 1862.

117 Letter from Colin Astbury in 1995.

118 *Worcester Chronicle*, 23 July 1862.

119 In June 1863.

120 *Southern Times and Dorset County Herald*, 3 June 1863.

121 *Salisbury and Winchester Journal*, 6 June 1863.

122 1863 Shropshire Directory.

123 In December 1866.

124 *Shrewsbury Chronicle*, 7 December 1866.

125 In November 1865.

126 *Eddowes Journal*, 12 December 1866.

Chapter Seven

127 *Staffordshire Advertiser*, 13 August 1864.

128 *Leamington Spa Courier*, 20 July 1867.

129 Haseley advowson papers, Worcester Record Office, 716.02/2536 v.

130 At Haseley on 28 March 1891.

131 *Leamington Spa Courier*, 10 October 1891.

132 Haseley advowson papers, Worcester Record Office, 716.02/2536 v.

Chapter Eight

133 Warwickshire White's Directory 1874.

134 http://www.warwickshirerailways.com/gwr/hattonstation.htm

135 https://www.british-history.ac.uk/vch/warks/vol3/pp104-108
136 https://www.british-history.ac.uk/vch/warks/vol3/pp104-108
137 Warwickshire White's Directory 1874.
138 *Warwick and Warwickshire Advertiser*, 20 October 1888.
139 *Warwick and Warwickshire Advertiser*, 7 September 1901.
140 *Leamington Spa Courier*, 27 September 1901.
141 *Leamington Spa Courier*, 22 November 1901.

Chapter Nine
142 *London Daily News* & *Liverpool Daily Post*, 27 September 1867.

Chapter Ten
143 *Cambrian News*, 16 May 1879.
144 *Cambrian News*, 16 May 1879.
145 *Public Ledger and Daily Advertiser*, 10 July 1869.
146 *Wrexham Guardian*, 20 November 1869.
147 *Wrexham Guardian*, 27 November 1869.
148 *Liverpool Mercury*, 27 November 1869.
149 On 5 March 1870.
150 *Chester Chronicle*, 5 March 1870.

Chapter Eleven
151 Will of Charles Bowdler Muckleston, dated 14 April 1799 and proved 14 May 1806. Prob 11/1443.
152 Chancery Document, reference C 16/513/M24 from the National Archives.
153 *Shipping and Mercantile Gazette*, 7 December 1869.
154 MI5546/2/10, document in Shropshire Archives.
155 Debtors Act 1869 – http://www.legislation.gov.uk/ukpga/Vict/32-33/62.
156 Held on 11 February 1870.
157 *Shrewsbury Chronicle*, 18 February 1870.
158 At the meeting held on 11 March 1870.
159 Loan made on 8 February 1868.
160 *Aris's Birmingham Gazette*, 12 March 1870.
161 On Wednesday 6 April 1870.
162 *Aris's Birmingham Gazette*, 9 April 1870.
163 25 March 1874.
164 MI5546/2/1, document at Shropshire Archives.
165 M15546/2/1, document at Shropshire Archives.
166 *Aris's Birmingham Gazette*, 22 October 1870.
167 On 26 April 1871.
168 In August 1870.
169 In March 1872.
170 *The Weekly Reporter Vol XX*, May 1872, page 619.
171 In November 1872.
172 Bishop of Worcester Sequestration Bonds, 737.5/2487/1.
173 In August 1878.

Chapter Twelve

174 Born December 1847.
175 On 21 May 1859.
176 Dated 9 February 1858 with a codicil dated 2 December 1858.
177 Will of Trafford Holmes.
178 Given name on the 1881 census.
179 On 24 November 1875.
180 On 12 May 1875.
181 *Leamington Spa Courier*, 26 July 1884.
182 On 27 July 1886.
183 *Warwick and Warwickshire Advertiser*, 21 August 1886.
184 *Leamington Spa Courier*, 11 January 1890.
185 Held in December 1889.
186 *Morning Post*, 14 June 1900.
187 On 21 December 1900.
188 *Chester Observer*, 22 December 1900.
189 *London Evening Standard*, 6 November 1883.
190 *Warwick and Warwickshire Advertiser*, 29 March 1884.
191 *Morning Post*, 18 July 1890.
192 *Bath Chronicle and Weekly Gazette*, 9 April 1891.

Chapter Thirteen

193 1871 census, RG10/3192/115.
194 Seebohm Rowntree's survey of York 1899.
195 *The Rise and Fall of the Victorian Servant*, Pamela Horn, Alan Sutton Publishing, 1996.
196 On Tuesday 23 March 1875.
197 https://www.theoldshirehall.co.uk/about
198 *Leamington Spa Courier*, 25 September 1875.
199 On Wednesday 29 March 1876.
200 *Leamington Spa Courier*, 20 January 1877.
201 On Tuesday 18 February.
202 *Leamington Spa Courier*, 17 February 1877.
203 *Western Daily Express*, 15 February 1877.
204 *Leamington Spa Courier*, 17 February 1877 and *Western Daily Press*, 15 February 1877.
205 On 18 January 1870.
206 *Leamington Spa Courier*, 27 April 1877.
207 In January 1881.
208 *Leamington Spa Courier*, 22 January 1881.
209 *Leamington Spa Courier*, 22 January 1881.
210 On Sunday 3 April 1881.
211 1881 UK Census, reference RG11/3088/8/8.
212 *Leamington Spa Courier*, 25 June 1881.
213 *Warwick and Warwickshire Advertiser*, 29 August 1885.
214 *Warwick and Warwickshire Advertiser*, 15 May 1886.

Chapter Fourteen

215 *Leamington Spa Courier*, 8 May 1875, coverage of a sports event on the same day.

216 www.warwickshirerailways.com, picture of the station in 1871.

217 *Leamington Spa Courier*, 12 June 1875.

218 *Bolton Evening News*, 7 June 1875.

219 *Secular Chronicle*, 1875.

Chapter Fifteen

220 *Leamington Spa Courier*, 29 January 1876.

221 *Leamington Spa Courier*, 30 September 1876.

222 *Birmingham Daily Post*, 16 May 1878.

223 *Leamington Spa Courier*, 16 November 1878.

224 *Leamington Spa Courier*, 14 December 1878.

225 Leamington Spa Courier 14 June 1879.

226 *Leamington Spa Courier*, 12 July 1879.

227 *Banbury Guardian*, 10 July 1884.

228 *Warwick and Warwickshire Advertiser*, 18 April 1885.

229 *Leamington Spa Courier*, 18 August 1888.

230 *Leamington Spa Courier*, 17 January 1891.

231 *Leamington Spa Courier*, 16 October 1897.

Chapter Sixteen

232 *Alcester Chronicle*, 29 June 1889.

233 http://www.workhouses.org.uk/

234 *Alcester Chronicle*, 3 May 1890.

235 *Alcester Chronicle*, 31 May 1890.

236 *Alcester Chronicle*, 12 July 1890.

237 Alcester Board of Guardians Meeting Minutes, June 1890, Warwickshire Archives, reference CR51/8.

Chapter Seventeen

238 *Warwick and Warwickshire Advertiser*, 23 September 1882.

239 *The Sportsman*, 6 September 1883.

240 *Leamington Spa Courier*, 11 July 1896.

241 During 1883 to 1884.

242 https://www.squire.law.cam.ac.uk/eminent-scholars-archiveprofessor-peter-stein/autobiography

243 *Lichfield Mercury*, 23 September 1898.

244 *Leamington Spa Courier*, 4 February 1899.

245 *Leamington Spa Courier*, 2 December 1899.

246 *Leamington Spa Courier*, 3 February 1900.

247 *Shrewsbury Chronicle*, 19 October 1900.

248 *Leamington Spa Courier*, 10 October 1902.

249 *Leamington Spa Courier*, 23 January 1903.

250 *Leamington Spa Courier*, 2 October 1903.

251 *Leamington Spa Courier*, 16 September 1904.
252 *Leamington Spa Courier*, 1 December 1905.
253 *Leamington Spa Courier*, 9 December 1904.
254 *Leamington Spa Courier*, 14 April 1905.
255 *Leamington Spa Courier*, 30 March 1906.
256 In April 1906.
257 *Leamington Spa Courier*, 9 November 1906.
258 *Shrewsbury Chronicle*, 22 July 1910.
259 https://www.britishsugar.co.uk/about-us/our-history

Chapter Eighteen
260 *British Medical Journal* Obituary, 1 February 1919.
261 *Birmingham Daily Post*, 18 March 1889.
262 On 10 June 1893.
263 *Leamington Spa Courier*, 18 June 1893.
264 *Leamington Spa Courier*, 28 November 1891.
265 *Grantham Journal*, 1 October 1892.
266 Will of Henry Cautley Holmes, proved 12 October 1892.
267 *Leamington Spa Courier*, 31 March 1894.
268 *Leamington Spa Courier*, 29 September 1894.
269 *Leamington Spa Courier*, 9 February 1895.
270 *Leamington Spa Courier*, 26 April 1901.
271 *Leamington Spa Courier*, 14 September 1895.
272 On Wednesday 12 August 1896.
273 *Leamington Spa Courier*, 15 August 1896.
274 *Leamington Spa Courier*, 24 July 1897.
275 *Leamington Spa Courier*, 25 September 1897.
276 *Leamington Spa Courier*, 11 September 1897.
277 On 11 November 1897.
278 In January 1899.
279 *Warwick and Warwickshire Advertiser*, 4 February 1899.
280 *Leamington Spa Courier*, 7 July 1900.
281 *Leamington Spa Courier*, 5 August 1899.
282 *Leamington Spa Courier*, 19 August 1899.
283 *Leamington Spa Courier*, 25 August 1905.
284 *Leamington Spa Courier*, 20 January 1900.
285 *Leamington Spa Courier*, 13 October 1900.
286 On Saturday 4 February 1901.
287 *Leamington Spa Courier*, 8 February 1901.
288 On 26 June 1902.
289 *Leamington Spa Courier*, 4 July 1902.
290 *Leamington Spa Courier*, 18 July 1902.
291 *Leamington Spa Courier*, 8 August 1902.
292 *Leamington Spa Courier*, 17 October 1902.
293 On Monday 13 April.
294 *Warwick and Warwickshire Advertiser*, 18 April 1903.

Chapter Nineteen

295 *Manchester Courier* and *Lancashire General Advertiser*, 8 June 1903.

296 *Leamington Spa Courier*, 17 July 1903.

297 *Warwick and Warwickshire Advertiser*, 18 July 1903.

298 *Leamington Spa Courier*, 28 October 1904.

299 *Leamington Spa Courier*, 22 January 1903.

300 *Leamington Spa Courier*, 11 March 1904.

301 *https://www.nationalarchives.gov.uk/humanrights*

302 Personal papers of Miss M. E. Muckleston, Warwick Record Office, reference CR3204/1.

303 *Leamington Spa Courier*, 1 April 1904.

304 *Leamington Spa Courier*, 22 and 29 April 1904.

305 Personal papers of Miss M. E. Muckleston Warwick Record Office, reference CR3204/1.

306 *Leamington Spa Courier*, 5 February 1904.

307 *Leamington Spa Courier*, 7 October 1904.

308 Haseley Parish baptism registers.

309 *Pall Mall Gazette*, 16 December 1904.

310 *Leamington Spa Courier*, 28 April 1905.

311 *Birmingham Daily Gazette*, 11 May 1905.

312 *Derbyshire Advertiser and Journal*, 2 June 1905.

313 *Leamington Spa Courier*, 4 August 1905.

314 *Leamington Spa Courier*, 9 June 1905.

315 *Leamington Spa Courier*, 28 September 1906.

316 *Leamington Spa Courier*, 3 April 1908.

317 *Leamington Spa Courier*, 11 September 1908.

318 *Leamington Spa Courier*, 15 December 1911.

319 *Derbyshire Advertiser and Journal*, 10 June 1910.

320 *Leamington Spa Courier*, 21 October 1910.

321 *Gloucester Citizen*, 12 September 1912.

322 *Warwick and Warwickshire Advertiser*, 11 October 1913.

323 *Leamington Spa Courier*, 28 November 1913.

324 *Leamington Spa Courier*, 5 December 1913.

Epilogue

325 A style of fashionable bag not necessarily made in Russia.

326 *Leamington Spa Courier*, 20 February 1914.

327 *Nantwich Guardian*, 20 April 1917.

328 *Yorkshire Post* and *Leeds Intelligencer*, 15 January 1929.

329 *Leamington Spa Courier*, 22 April 1932.

330 Will of Charles Edward Muckleston, proved 19 August 1932.

331 *Warwick and Warwickshire Advertiser*, 29 April 1933.

332 On 5 August 1936.

333 *Leamington Spa Courier*, 7 August 1936.

334 *Leamington Spa Courier*, 31 December 1937.

335 *Gloucestershire Echo*, 6 February 1940.

336 *Coventry Evening Telegraph*, 2 November 1949.
337 *Leamington Spa Courier*, 4 November 1949.
338 Will of Louisa Gwendoline Muckleston.
339 *Staffordshire Advertiser*, 1 August 1952.
340 *Rugby Advertiser*, 24 April 1953.
341 *Birmingham Daily Post*, 21 June 1974.
342 *Birmingham Daily Post*, 16 December 1960.
343 *Birmingham Daily Post*, 22 March 1967.
344 *Coventry Evening Telegraph*, 31 May 1968.
345 *Birmingham Daily Post*, 21 June 1974.
346 Will of John Corbet Muckleston.
347 Will of Dorothy Amy Muckleston.